ASKIWINA

ASKIWINA

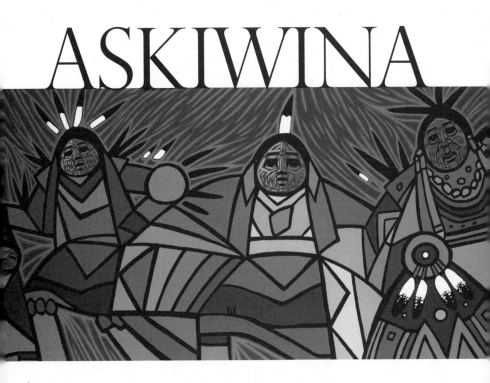

A · CREE · WORLD

DOUG · CUTHAND

Edited by Roberta Mitchell Coulter.
Cover image: "Untitled II" by Gerry Whitehead.
Interior illustrations by Gerry Whitehead.
Cover and book design by Duncan Campbell.
Printed and bound in Canada by Marquis Bookprinting.
This book is printed on 100% recycled paper.

Library and Archives Canada Cataloguing in Publication

Cuthand, Doug
    Askiwina : a Cree world / Doug Cuthand.

ISBN 978-1-55050-345-6

1. Indians of North America—Canada—History.
2. Indians of North America—Canada—Social life and customs.
3. Indians of North America—Canada—Biography. I. Title.

E78.C2C899 2007   971.004'97   C2007-902370-3X

10 9 8 7 6 5 4 3 2 1

2517 Victoria Avenue
Regina, Saskatchewan
Canada S4P 0T2

Available in Canada & the US from
Fitzhenry & Whiteside
195 Allstate Parkway
Markham, ON, Canada L3R 4T8

The publisher gratefully acknowledges the financial assistance of the Saskatchewan Arts Board, the Canada Council for the Arts, the Government of Canada through the Book Publishing Industry Development Program (BPIDP), the Association for the Export of Canadian Books, the Multicultural Initiative Fund of SaskCulture and the City of Regina Arts Commission, for its publishing program.

For our son, Christopher

CONTENTS

INTRODUCTION

The history of the First Nations of the Great Plains is overlooked in Canadian history. At school we learned about the fur trade and the building of the railway, but the First Nations were only given passing reference. In reality, the early explorers followed routes long established by First Nations, not discovering the West but being treated as its first tourists. The fur trade was built on the backs of the First Nations trappers, and the railway and western Canada wouldn't have existed if the First Nations had not signed treaties with the Crown.

Reading history is a painful experience for First Nations people because we are so poorly regarded. It seems that everything from pre-Columbian history to the history that unfolds daily in our newspapers carries a point of view different from our own.

When I compiled my first book, *Tapwe,* I left out stories related to history and First Nations legends and spirituality. My intention was to save them for a future book. I felt they needed a special place and should be treated as such.

These stories are not mine. I am only a storyteller. The stories belong to our people and have been handed down to me through my father and other elders. Many of my stories came from my father, who received them from his father, and they in turn were handed down to him.

My grandfather died before I was born, but he passed his stories along to his children and Dad passed them along to me. My grandfather was born in the early 1870s, and he remembered the last of the buffalo hunts, the battle at Cutknife Hill, and the subsequent journey to the United States to escape the repression following the "rebellion" of 1885. These stories have been passed on to me and they are part of this book.

My family has a long history of service to our people. My great-grandfather, Misatimwas, was a headman to Chief Little Pine. My grandfather was a band councillor under our band's last lifetime chief, Blackman. My father served the Chiefs at La Ronge and Ahtahkakoop and assisted in the formation of the Federation of Saskatchewan Indians. I served as a Vice-Chief of the Federation of Saskatchewan Indian Nations and as a trustee for my First Nation.

It has not been our desire to aspire to leadership, but rather to work with the leaders and stay in the background. They say a journalist is a shy egotist, and it's a definition that suits me fine.

Unfortunately, leadership over the years has not seen my role in the same light. Criticism of leadership is regarded as heresy in the First Nations political world. Criticism is seen as treason, and it has been emphasized to me that since we receive enough criticism from the media we don't need our own people "stabbing us in the back."

Historically, our leaders took a lot of criticism from their own people, and this continues today at Band meetings and other venues. Today our people are also media savvy and read newspapers and watch television. These are tools that we must use to educate our people. Public discussion and public debate are important to us and can't be left to an elite few.

Newspapers chronicle the events of our time, and a columnist should present the reasons behind and effects of contemporary events. We need to move on to debate the issues in a mature and reasoned forum.

This book travels from the past to the present. It gives the reader a glimpse of our past and our beliefs, in the hope that this will help people understand the present.

"Askiwina" is a Cree word that refers to the passage of time, roughly meaning "over the years." An elder once described her life on a reserve close to a city. The city grew up to the reserve boundaries but her people remained. "I'm still here," she told me.

That comment sums up First Nations in Canada. We're still here.

CHAPTER ONE

THE LAND IS OUR SOUL

Our people believe that the earth and all the creatures that live on it are a gift from the Creator. This beautiful land of lakes, forests, rivers, plains, and mountains is a gift from the Almighty and it must be respected and treated properly.

The Almighty prepared this land for us, and the hand of the Almighty guides the earth through the seasons.

The Four Directions

First Nations culture and religion rely heavily on the belief in the power and mystery of the four directions. This belief is ingrained in our prayers and the way we look at the earth.

The honouring of the four directions is universal among the First Nations of the plains and woodlands. There are, however, variations among the different cultural groups. I am of the Cree nation, so I have been taught from that point of view.

The symbol of the four directions is shown in paintings, on tipis, in beadwork, and in other artistic media. The symbols of four arrows are used to depict the four directions. In addition, the number four is sacred, and many ceremonies are repeated four times in order to worship each of the four directions.

The story of the four directions, also known as the four winds, is that they are brothers, and, like brothers, they sometimes fight among themselves.

There are two other brothers who were created to help the people: Flint and Rabbit. Flint gave the people the gift of fire, and Rabbit gave the gift of food. The Almighty told the people that in times of famine and shortage of food there would always be rabbits for the people to eat.

The North is represented by the colour white and is called Kewatin. Kewatin is a cold, fierce northern wind that brings us winter. Kewatin was the brother who wanted to rule the world, and when he was denied this power, he turned against the earth and came south and ravaged the land every year.

The South is represented by yellow and is known as Sawin, or the healing wind. Sawin and Kewatin don't get along and they affect the land as they fight and force each other in one direction or the other.

The changes in the seasons are explained by the fighting of these two brothers. Kewatin will come storming down from the north in the autumn and chase Sawin to the south. Sawin in return will take the ducks, geese, and other waterfowl with him to protect them from the ravages of the coming winter. Other animals such as the bear and small ground animals like gophers and groundhogs will go away and sleep, waiting for Sawin's return. Kewatin will then freeze the land, bringing with him the great herds of caribou to feed the people during the winter.

In a few months, Kewatin will be tired and spent from all the cold and storms he must create. Then Sawin will once again gain the upper hand and come back and chase the weaker Kewatin to the north. Kewatin will travel north and spend the summer months resting up for his journey to the south and another battle with his brother Sawin.

Sawin is also called the healing wind because he heals the land, brings new life, and allows the birds return to raise their young before Kewatin returns from the far north. The eastern Arctic is known as the district of Kewatin in honour of the place where the North Wind lives.

The other two directions are also very important because they regulate the length of the days and are the keepers of the sun.

The East Wind, or Wapun, keeps the sun and releases it every morning for its journey across the heavens. The East is represented by the colour red. If you watch the sun come up, you will see the red in the clouds. In Cree, *Wapun* means the dawn of a new day.

The West, or Nepawanuk, takes the sun each night and returns it to the East so a new day will dawn. *Nepawanuk* is a Cree word meaning "the place where the sun goes down." It is represented by the colour black.

The West is a very kindly direction. Nepawanuk made a promise that he would look after the dead, so the West is the destination for people when they die and go to the spirit world. The West is the keeper of the spirits. The West also provides a constant wind that dries the land. At one time, the West Wind scolded his brother Wapun and told him that both good and bad could come from the East and he must be vigilant. The prophecy would come true with the arrival of the Europeans, who brought both good and bad.

These four directions are honoured for their gifts to humankind. Each one brings with it gifts that people can use, but the givers of gifts must be honoured and their contribution recognized. When we have our pipe ceremonies, the pipe is pointed in the four directions and a prayer is given to each direction. The same thing holds true for the sweat lodge. Four prayers are given to the four directions, and, after each, the rocks are sprinkled with water. When people go on a fast, it lasts four days to honour each of the four directions. A sundance lasts four days, and if a person hosts a sundance he must host it four times. Later, when the government outlawed the sundance, it was only held for one and a half days because of fear that it would be shut down.

One summer I heard a beautiful story.
A young man had died before his time. The funeral party was passing a pasture on the way to the graveyard. As they passed the pasture, four horses appeared and stood quietly beside the fence. One was a sorrel, or red, another was a palomino, or yellow, and the other two were black and white – the colours of the four directions. The four horses walked along the fence line following the mourners.

When the family saw the four horses they knew in their hearts that the spirits had come to take the young man's spirit home to the West.

The four directions represent an important part of our history and culture. They explain the seasons, they contain teachings to make us a stronger people, and they help to heal the wounds of our people.

The Creation Story – Wesakechak

The West Wind had a son named Wesakechak. Wesakechak was a young man who often got in trouble. One day he was on the coast when he spied some baby seals. He got closer and killed one with his spear. The other seals got very angry and caused waves in the ocean that flooded the land.

Wesakechak was forced to flee for his life. He built a raft to save himself from drowning. A beaver and a muskrat climbed on board, and soon they were joined by other animals.

Wesakechak and his new companions were trapped on the raft in the middle of a great sea. There was no land, the world was only water. The Creator told Wesakechak that since he had outraged the seals and caused the flood, he would have to create a new world.

In order to create the world they first had to obtain some earth that could be used as the foundation. First the beaver dove to the bottom, but although he was gone for a long time, he came up without any dirt. The poor beaver was almost drowned, and Wesakechak thought it was hopeless.

The little muskrat asked if he could try. At first Wesakechak thought it was beyond his ability, but the muskrat insisted, so Wesakechak let him dive. The brave little animal dove in and swam as far down as he could. He was gone for a long time, and when he came to the surface he told Wesakechak that he had not found the bottom.

He tried again but was still unsuccessful. Wesakechak paddled the raft to another location, but still the little muskrat was unable to find the bottom of the sea.

On the fourth try, the muskrat took several deep breaths, filling his lungs, and dove to the bottom with all his might. He was gone for a very long time, and Wesakechak began to worry for his little friend. Finally he broke the surface. He was more dead than alive, and Wesakechak had to revive him. But this time he held a small amount of dirt in his hand.

Wesakechak took the small handful of dirt and blew on it. The dirt began to grow, and after a little while it became a small island. Wesakechak continued to blow on it and it grew and grew until Wesakechak could no longer see the end of it. The land continued to grow, and it became known as Turtle Island.

Wesakechak then began the task of creating all the animals that walked, flew, slithered, or swam. All the animals picked out their place.

The First Nations creation story is one of trial and error, and the individual features of each animal exist because of accident or design on the part of Wesakechak. Stories are told of the different animals and how they interacted with each other or how they developed strange characteristics. This creation story is rather humorous and reflects the irreverence of the First Nations.

Wesakechak was a person with human weaknesses and a sense of humour, and many of his creations reflected this. When Wesakechak had finished creating all the animals of the earth, he looked around and found some spare parts that hadn't been used. He found a large coat of long dark hair. There was a large nose, two floppy ears, some long legs, and a set of large flat antlers. He took these odds and ends and created the last animal. He wasn't sure what it was, but after he got it together he gave it life, and it walked around admiring itself. The animal was a moose, and he was very proud of the way he looked. He had a beautiful black coat, two wonderful ears, tall legs, and a lovely rack of flat antlers.

He went down to the lake and admired his reflection in the water, and he was very pleased. But the other animals were not so kind. They laughed at him and called him ugly and clumsy. They made fun of his flat antlers and large nose.

Moose was devastated. He thought that he looked just fine, and here were all the other animals laughing at him. Nobody was perfect: Rabbit with his long ears and big feet, Beaver with his funny flat tail and large teeth, and Pelican with his large bill. Why should they laugh at him when they looked just as funny?

But poor Moose continued to be teased and laughed at by the other animals. So he told them, "I will go away and live in dark swampy places all by myself." And so he went deep into the forest and lived by himself in dark, damp places.

Today, if you want to find a moose, you have to go into the forest and find a secluded swampy area. He lives alone and doesn't even associate with members of his own kind, unlike other large animals that live in herds like the elk or caribou.

This story is told so the children can see the damage that teasing and prejudice have on other people. In this case, he was only a moose, but he had feelings, and it changed his way of life forever. It is also a story of tolerance towards people from other races and backgrounds. Racism hurts, and those who suffer its sting often want to withdraw from the world and go somewhere they can be themselves.

The reaction of Moose to prejudice was normal and his story serves as a lesson to us all.

Sometimes Wesakechak would be called upon for advice. One of his creations was a beautiful bird with grey and black feathers. The bird was very unhappy and he told Wesakechak, "I have a large head and small wings. I can only fly from tree to tree. When the cold weather comes I will be unable to fly south with all the other birds."

Wesakechak thought for a while and told the bird to go and live with the people and they would take care of him.

The bird flew to a camp where the people were staying and sat on a branch. Soon a woman appeared and set out some food for him. He gratefully accepted it, and from then on the bird, whom the people called Weskaypoo, was a friend to the people. Wherever the people travelled in the forest, Weskaypoo would follow and watch over them. In return, the people would leave out some food for the bird.

Later, when other people from far away came to live in the same land, they couldn't pronounce the name. They called Weskaypoo "whisky-jack."

Not every one of the creations was a success, however. At one time, the Indian people of North America lived together with a race of giants. The giants thought that because of their size, they could always do what they pleased and get what they wanted. These large beings abused the earth, killed more animals than they needed, and attacked the people for no reason. They thought that they didn't have to answer to anybody.

One day Wesakechak visited the giants. He told them that they would have to leave and live by themselves because they had broken the rule of living in harmony with nature and humanity. They had not respected the gifts that the Creator had given them and so they had to move to the deepest part of the mountains.

At first the giants didn't want to leave because they still thought that they were invincible, but Wesakechak took away their power, and they left and travelled to the mountains.

Today, some of the descendants of the giants still exist. They are known as "Bigfoot" or "Sasquatch." They live alone in the mountains and hide from people. They continue to pay for the sins of their forefathers.

This story is told to teach our people to respect the earth and the gifts from the Creator. We don't have "dominion" over the earth like western thought proclaims. We are one with nature because we are no better or worse than the animals, trees, and rocks. It's a philosophy that needs to be practised more as we move into a period of climate change and eco-crises.

The stories of the creation of the world and its beings illustrate the humour and imagination of our people. The animals may have their faults and shortcomings, but the stories provide an explanation. In our mythology and religion, people are part of nature, and the Creator was very human.

There are many, many stories of Wesakechak, and they can be found in other books. However, these stories are only to be told in the winter when the hard work is done and people need entertainment for the long winter nights. If you tell these stories in the summer, your home will be overrun with lizards, frogs, and rodents. This is our people's way of making sure that everyone works hard during the summer, putting up food for the winter, breaking camp, and travelling to good hunting grounds.

The Sundance

June 21 is the summer solstice – the longest day of the year. This is considered the most sacred time of the year, and it is the time for the annual sundances.

First Nations people are monotheistic. We believe in one God. This God is manifested in the world around us, and the life-giving sun is part of that. Some people have the mistaken idea that we worship the sun. This is simplistic – we worship the Almighty who created the sun. When the missionaries converted our people to Christianity, it wasn't such a great leap in philosophy, and even today people move back and forth between the two. A person may participate in a "pagan" ceremony one day and be in church the next.

Unfortunately, the government didn't take the same liberal view, and the sundance and other important ceremonies such as the West Coast potlatch were outlawed in the Indian Act. Across the prairies and on the West Coast, people were actually sent to jail for practising their religion. The ceremonies were considered dangerous and a threat to the policy of civilizing the Indians. The sundances were held in the summer after the children were sent home from residential schools, and the government feared that one pagan ritual would upset the whole year's work with the new generation. With the government and the missionaries, it had to be complete control.

The sundance is the most sacred of all the rituals. People taking part don't do so lightly. It means months of preparation; vows must be made. In some cases it can be an expression of thanks-giving. If someone has had their life or the life of a loved one spared during the year, participation in the sundance is a necessary act.

During the winter months, singers will practise the sacred sundance songs in preparation for the event.

When the sundance was outlawed, it was a serious break with a tradition that was as old as the prairies. It was a key ceremony in an ancient religion. The need to conduct the sundance was too strong, and it continued in secluded areas hidden from the prying eyes of the RCMP and the Indian agents.

During the 1930s on my reserve, my grandfather and several other men from the community went to town and met with the Indian agent to ask for permission to hold a sundance. The request was denied, and they went home empty-handed.

They decided to proceed anyway. The sundance lodge was erected on the north side of the reserve across the Battle River in thick bush.

Meanwhile, in town, the RCMP officer heard that the sundance was taking place and the Indian agent sent him out to put a stop to it. But when he arrived on the reserve, he failed to find any sign of the sundance, or anything else for that matter.

Finally he discovered that it was being held across the river, and he set off. However, his car slipped into a deep mud hole and got hopelessly stuck. He couldn't get it out, and he couldn't find anyone to help him. He ended up walking back to town for help. The sundance continued.

For years the annual sundance was held in secret and hidden away from view. Other more social events like powwows were open to the general public, but the sundance was held in seclusion. Our people practised their religion with quiet dignity in a state of nonviolent resistance.

Today the sundance is more public, but it is still an intensely personal act of faith. We are still not allowed to photograph these ceremonies, a holdover from when people feared that they would get in trouble for practising the old ways. This ban is a vestige of our colonial past, and it continues into the present.

A sundance takes place over four days. Four is a sacred number that signifies the four winds, the four directions, the four sacred colours, and so on. Over a period of four days, people who participate must neither eat nor drink during the day. Some fast the entire time; others will have water when the sun goes down.

The longest day of the year has now been officially declared Aboriginal Day by the federal government. The day was chosen in consultation with Aboriginal groups because of its cultural and historical significance. But more importantly, the sundance has made a spectacular comeback, and our people are able to worship unmolested.

Landmarks and Sacred Places

The First Nations of the plains saw beauty and spirituality in the land. The land was their mother, so there were important places that were regarded as sacred and special. Heading north from the Cypress Hills along the Alberta – Saskatchewan border, there are a series of sacred places.

The Cypress Hills are important to our people. These great hills that rise out of the flat plain were a sanctuary, a hunting ground, and a sacred place. No one tribe claimed ownership of the hills, and during the winter many nations would gather in safety and comfort there. The hills were international territory, and all were safe.

Our people spent their winters in the Cypress Hills; during the summer they would head out onto the Great Plains and hunt buffalo. They would either head south into the Bear Paw Mountains in Montana, or they would go north as far as the North Saskatchewan River. When they made the trip north they would follow a series of landmarks.

North from the Cypress Hills are the Great Sand Hills. These spectacular sand dunes on the flat prairie were one of the places where the spirits dwelt. People seeking guidance and enlightenment would go to the sand hills for a vision quest. A vision quest was a ceremony conducted by one or sometimes two people. The quest was a way to reach out to the spirits and receive an answer or insight into an important question.

A little further north, close to the Alberta border, is Bull's Forehead, a butte or hill located where the Red Deer and South Saskatchewan rivers join. Early people would go to pray at the top of the butte. It was an important landmark for the people of the plains because two great rivers joined there. In Cree, the river is called the *waskesieu sippi* or "Elk River" (which is where the Red Deer River gets its name) until it joins up with the North Saskatchewan River east of Prince Albert.

Further north lie Sounding Lake and Manitou Lake. These lakes are sacred in Aboriginal mythology and are considered places where the spirits dwell. Manitou Lake, located near the Alberta border west of the Battlefords, has a long and rich history in both First Nations spirituality and the more recent history of our people. The name *Manitou* means God, the Almighty, or a great secret. In this case, the name refers to the great secret of the spirits that dwell within the lake.

According to legend, many years ago a group of people were crossing the lake in winter. Somewhere near the middle of the lake they found a horn sticking out of the ice. They started to chop it out and discovered that it was the horn of a huge snake that lived in the lake. These were the snakes that did battle with the thunderbirds and pulled them under the water. When the huge snake was freed from the ice, it thrashed around, pulling the people under the ice, where they all died. Manitou Lake became known as a place of great mystery where the spirits dwelt.

The battles between the enormous lake snakes and the thunderbirds are an important source of First Nations legends. Southwest of Manitou Lake in Alberta is a lake where a thunderbird was pulled in and killed by a huge snake. On a still night, one can hear the plaintive cry of the thunderbird. This gives the lake the name "Sounding Lake."

Manitou Lake remained a special place, and future generations of Indian people camped close by and warriors visited while on a vision quest. My great-grandfather Misatimwas and Chief Paspaschase also went to the lake to conduct their vision quest.

Young men went on a vision quest to seek inner strength and commune with the spirits. Older men who went on a vision quest did so in search of answers to very specific issues. Misatimwas and Paspaschase were searching for answers to combat the plagues that were decimating the Indian population.

Around the turn of the nineteenth century, the grassland around the lake was settled by Cree and Saulteaux families who raised horses and sold them to the white settlers. They were considered a good source of horses, and the settlers were eager to do business.

For years the people lived around Manitou Lake thinking that their grasslands were safe from white settlers. The land held no reserve status, but they felt that they owned it because of their long occupancy. In the 1940s, the provincial government seized the land for a community pasture. The people were dispersed to various reserves, including Sweetgrass and Little Pine. A few moved away to the Sunchild reserve located north of Rocky Mountain House in Alberta. But the majority of the people were resettled on the newly created Saulteaux reserve north of the Battlefords. The Manitou Lake community pasture still contains old cellars and building sites from the days when it was Indian land. There is also at least one graveyard.

Recently, there has been oil exploration in the area, and people from local reserves are assisting by identifying historic sites and pointing out which areas are to be avoided.

All these landmarks north of the Cypress Hills still exist, but we can only remember the place where the Iron Creek meteorite once lay.

The Iron Creek meteorite fell to earth long before the arrival of the Europeans, and for many years this was a place of worship and reverence. The meteorite was located to the west of the Alberta border about sixteen kilometres from the Battle River. It was probably located on a hill known locally as Strawstack Hill. About twenty years ago, gravel was removed from the hill and human remains were unearthed. The pit was shut down because it was believed that Aboriginal peoples used the area for important burials.

The meteorite itself weighs about 175 kilograms and is over 91 percent iron and 8 percent nickel, with the remainder consisting of trace elements.

It was known by the First Nations people as the Manitou Stone after the Almighty because it contained the clear outline of the profile of a man's face.

For years, various tribes would visit the site and leave offerings to the Almighty. They believed that the meteor fell to earth as a sign from the Almighty that the people would be cared for and be free from famine and disease.

In 1866, the Reverend John McDougall, a Methodist missionary, removed the meteorite. He believed that it was an evil pagan instrument. If the Indians were to be Christianized and civilized, all vestiges of their pagan past had to be removed.

The people saw the removal of the stone as a sacrilege. The medicine men and elders foretold that with the loss of the Manitou Stone, they would suffer three disasters: plague, the loss of the buffalo herds and resulting famine, and war.

The winter of 1867–68 was extremely harsh, and the following year the buffalo hunt failed. In 1870, the first of a series of smallpox epidemics swept through the area. It is estimated that the smallpox epidemic killed half the people on the plains. That same year, war broke out between the Cree and Blackfoot.

For years to come, the people spoke of the sacrilegious behaviour of the white men. McDougall thought it would force the Indians closer to the church, but in fact it had the opposite effect.

The meteorite was taken to Winnipeg and later to Victoria College in Toronto, where it was placed near the door of the college's chapel. For years it sat there as a trophy of colonialism. When Victoria College was amalgamated with the University of Toronto, it was moved to the Royal Ontario Museum, where it languished in obscurity.

In 1972, the meteorite was returned to Alberta, where it now sits in a position of prominence in the Provincial Museum in Edmonton. There is a move among First Nations people to have the meteorite sent back to its original location, or at least treated as the sacred object it is.

Two mysteries remain about the meteorite.

First, the last great herd of buffalo on the plains was seen in the Iron Creek area. Elders said that the buffalo were searching for the sacred stone.

Second, the legend states that when the sacred stone was first found it was the size of a man's fist and that it grew over the years. Elders spoke of lifting it easily when they were young but finding it much heavier when they were older. In fact, it took two men to lift it. McDougall estimated its weight at 200 pounds (90 kilograms). Today it is reported to weigh about 175 kilograms, or 386 pounds.

Legends abound about the sacred stone. One is that it fell to earth and landed somewhere else. It was carried to the hilltop to be closer to the heavens it came from. Another legend states that after the sacred stone was stolen, another meteorite was taken and placed in Lac Ste. Anne to the west of Edmonton.

The "stone who fell from the sky" is an important part of our spirituality. Its loss to our people has only made remembering it more important.

Powwow Time

Another part of our cultural revitalization is the growth of gatherings such as the powwow. Summer in Indian Country is powwow time. This is the time of year when people gather on the weekends, meet old friends, and make new ones. In the winter there are special powwows such as a Christmas powwow and one honouring veterans. The powwow is an event unique to the First Nations, and it illustrates our cultural and economic differences.

To begin with, a powwow is free. There are no admission fees, camping fees, or any other charges. The idea is that people attending the powwow are guests and must be treated as such.

If a First Nation is planning to put on a powwow it must raise funds for about a year in advance. The powwow committee is a permanent fixture on most reserves, as planning and fund raising are a year-round activity. The guests receive free camping, water, firewood, and a bag of "rations" each day. Some First Nations will butcher a cow and distribute the meat. Others will send out a hunting party for deer or moose meat. In addition, the drum groups must be paid and prize money given to the top dancers. Nobody ever made money holding a powwow.

This is the opposite of fairs and exhibitions that are held in other communities. These celebrations are designed to make money or at least break even. This is a reflection of a different economic mindset. A powwow, on the other hand, costs money and by definition cannot make money. This is also an example of Aboriginal philosophy.

There are, of course, times when a special dance will be held to show support to a family that has suffered a loss, such as a house fire or death in the family. This is called a blanket dance. Four of the organizers will hold an outstretched blanket and the affected family will follow behind as the blanket is carried around the circle. People will toss money into the blanket to provide some support to the family.

Time is another factor where a powwow stands out. Nobody seems to be in a hurry. For a weekend powwow, people will begin to arrive on Thursday or Friday and set up their camps, get comfortable, and visit. There may be a hand game – a form of Indian gambling – or two.

Today we have powwow trail that extends across the prairies and into the United States. The border didn't exist in the past, and each year our people still travel south to visit friends and relations. The powwow trail offers a wonderful opportunity to keep these historic and traditional bonds alive.

For example, my family has relations at Rocky Boy and the Crow reservation in Montana. These relationships predate the reservation system and are very important to us.

If you want to visit a powwow, you will find that you are welcome. There are two types of powwows, traditional and contemporary. The contemporary powwow offers dance competitions, while there are no competitions at a traditional powwow. Each powwow has its appeal.

The powwow will start with the grand entry, where all the dancers and dignitaries will enter the dancing area and officially open the powwow. The grand entry is followed by dancing and dance competitions that will continue until about one or two in the morning. There is no real agenda. Competitions follow the routine of women and children first, with the spectacular men's fancy dancers finishing off the evening.

At a contemporary powwow, the competitions can be spectacular. Prize money can amount to serious cash. It all culminates in the fall at the world championships at the Pequot reservation in Connecticut.

On the morning of the second day there is a "give away," when groups and families present gifts to those who have come from other reserves. The tradition of giving is a special part of all First Nations cultures. On the West Coast, the potlatch ceremony is another example of an event where people gave gifts to each other. The Dene, Inuit, and other First Nations have similar practices. At one time, even poor individuals gave away blankets, rifles, and horses. Friendships were valued more than property. These acts of selfless giving so confused the white people that the potlatch was actually outlawed in the Indian Act.

The dancing categories reflect the changes in our culture as we evolve and grow. In the men's categories, the traditional dancers are usually older men who prefer the less strenuous style. The grass dancers, with their long fringes, represent the waves of grass on the limitless prairie. The fancy dancers are the young men who represent strength and athletic ability.

The women also have traditional dancers and fancy dancers, but in place of the grass dancers they have the jingle dress dancers. These women wear dresses that are covered in rows and rows of cone-shaped bells. The bells jingle musically as they dance.

All the different types of dancers attend traditional powwows too, but there are no competitions. People participate for the shear joy of experiencing the culture and the dance.

The second important part of the powwow is the drum groups. These groups compete both formally and informally, and many of the top groups put out their own albums. The drum is the heartbeat of the earth, and the sound resonates across the camp. It is what unites us and makes us strong.

The powwow is our celebration, but is open to everyone who wants to come and enjoy themselves. You don't have to be an Indian to have fun at a powwow.

Profile – Canon Edward Ahenakew

The roots of First Nations resistance and political organizing go deep in our past. One of our unsung heroes is Canon Edward Ahenakew.

Edward Ahenakew was born in 1885 and died in 1961. During his lifetime, he saw his people begin the early stages of political development, and he played an important role.

He was the first educated member of the Ahtahkakoop reserve. He went to Emmanuel College in Prince Albert. The college was a boarding school established in the 1880s to train teachers and pastors for the Church of England.

In 1903, Edward graduated with his senior matriculation and taught school on the John Smith reserve. Later, he decided to go into the ministry, and in 1912, he graduated from Emmanuel College, which by then was a part of the new University of Saskatchewan in Saskatoon.

He moved to the Onion Lake reserve and served the people there for several years. In 1918, there was an influenza pandemic that was brought home by soldiers returning from the First World War. Indian people were especially hard hit, and Onion Lake was no exception. In a report at the time, he described the scene: "The church was piled high with bodies. On the reserves so many people were dying that mass funerals and burials were being held."

The epidemic took a terrible toll. By 1920, the Indian population was at an all-time low. According to the Indian Department's annual report of 1920, there were about 105,000 Indians left in the whole dominion.

In those tragic times, Ahenakew decided to study medicine so he could be of greater use to his people. He took a leave of absence and moved to Edmonton, where he studied medicine at the University of Alberta.

This was before the days of government educational assistance, so he did it on his own. He was forced to drop out after three years because his poverty had led to malnutrition. He left medical school exhausted and sick.

He returned to Saskatchewan, and after a period of convalescence he returned to the ministry. He moved to Fort a la Corne (the old name for the James Smith First Nation, east of Prince Albert).

During the 1930s, the League of Indians was formed to speak on behalf Indian people nationally. It was started by Frederick Ogilvie Loft, a Mohawk veteran of the First World War. The organization was short-lived, but it sowed the seeds for future Indian organizations. Loft was branded an agitator by the Indian Department and placed under police surveillance.

In 1932 Edward Ahenakew was elected vice-president of the league for western Canada. He travelled to Ottawa as a part of his duties and met with senior officials of the department. The reception was hostile, and the

Indians were treated like criminals. The government officials complained to the church, and the bishop told Ahenakew to attend to his duties and not meddle with the affairs of the state. In 1933 Ahenakew tendered his resignation at a meeting of the league at Poundmaker. He was replaced by John Tootoosis.

But Ahenakew remained a spokesman for his people. He lived on the James Smith reserve until his retirement in 1955. He lived in poverty and never married. He devoted his life to his work and his people.

He was a prolific writer, and following his death his manuscripts were discovered and printed in a book called Voices of the Plains Cree. He chronicled the old stories because he feared that the past would soon die and young people would lose their history.

Edward Ahenakew was the first in a series of political and spiritual leaders that worked within the church to help their people on a broad level. Like the early leaders of the civil rights movement in the United States, Ahenakew was able to speak out and use the resources of the church to further the progress of his people.

Edward Ahenakew was our Martin Luther King.

CHAPTER TWO

HISTORY
AS WE SEE IT

First Nations' attitudes towards newcomers to their land was mixed. When the first settlers arrived, they were generally treated with polite suspicion. This was misconstrued as putting out the welcome mat. Trading relations were established, and the newcomers' technology was welcomed. However, our ancestors soon found out that technology came at a price. The price was disease, repression, and loss of our land.

Settling the Americas

The First Nations reaction to and attitude towards the new-comers has been mixed. When the first settlers arrived, they were generally treated with polite suspicion. This was miscon-strued as putting out the welcome mat. Trading relations were established, and the newcomers' technology was welcomed. However, our ancestors soon found out that the technology came with a price. The price was disease, repression, and loss of our land.

Pastoral scenes such as the first Thanksgiving show the Indians and Pilgrims sitting down at the same table. This image continues to persist as part of the collective mythology that the land was settled and shared peacefully.

In reality, the Pilgrims almost starved to death, and the Indian tribes helped them out with their own produce, such as beans, squash, and corn. They also showed the Pilgrims how to hunt wild turkey and other animals. The Indians spent the winter in nice cosy longhouses and wigwams while the Pilgrims froze in crude shelters. Without the help of the Indians, the Pilgrims would have made no progress.

Aboriginal people taught early explorers and settlers how to survive. Medicines from rat root, red willow, and other plants were valuable painkillers. When the French army was afflicted with scurvy at Quebec City, local Indians showed them how to prepare a medicinal tea of dried berries and spruce bows to combat it.

And there are lots of stories, some as recent as the Depression of the 1930s, when Indian people helped farmers caught in crop failure and poverty.

Foods developed and cultivated by the First Nations of the New World were taken and spread around the world and adopted by others. The Irish potato came from the Andes; tomatoes from Mexico were cultivated in Italy; corn was called maize by the British and became the staple food of Africa.

In return, the colonizers enslaved the local tribes and made them work the gold mines and plantations until they either died of exhaustion and disease or simply ran away. When they ran out of Indians, they were forced to go to Africa for a fresh supply of slaves.

The great epidemics that swept across the continent were among the most traumatic and soul-destroying events in human history. Our skewed European view of the world points to the Black Death of Europe as one of the world's greatest plagues, but it pales in comparison to the death that swept across the Americas. It is estimated that the Black Death killed one-third of the inhabitants of Europe; the smallpox epidemic, on the other hand, killed an estimated half of the Aboriginal population on the prairies.

Over the years, there has been a school of thought in the First Nations world that someday the old way of life would return. Near the end of the last century, the Ghost Dance religion flourished on the plains. They believed that the buffalo would return and the white people would go away. The battle at Wounded Knee was the United States Army's way of dealing with what they thought was an insurrection. In reality, it was something more potent. It was the belief that the spirits of the dead would return and bring with them the old way of life.

When I was in South America, I went to Cuzco, Peru. Cuzco is the ancient capital of the Incan Empire and is surrounded by some of the most magnificent archaeological remains in the hemisphere. When the Spanish built their cathedral, they built it on top of the Incan temple to the sun. The last Incan emperor is entombed under the bell tower.

They have a legend that someday the Inca will rise up and claim back the Incan Empire. Earlier in the last century, Cuzco was hit with an earthquake and the bell tower swayed precariously. A large crowd gathered in anticipation of the rebirth of the Inca.

The rebirth of the Indian nations is a theme that persists today but it is viewed in light of existing circumstances. The prophesies of the seventh fire or the fifth generation call for the rebirth of the culture and religion after a defined period of time. In most cases, this period is upon us now. The prophesies state that the Indian nations will once again become great and take their rightful place among the nations of the earth. This theme persists throughout the Americas, and in some ways it is coming true. Aboriginal people hold political office in many Canadian jurisdictions. The election of Evo Morales in Bolivia is another example of Indigenous people taking their rightful place.

The Fur Trade

History can be very different depending on who is telling it. Napoleon said that history was a group of lies agreed upon. One of the myths out there in Indian Country is how long we have inhabited this land. Political hacks like to posture and state that "We have lived here since 'time immemorial'." Of course they are believed – they said it and therefore it must be true. They like to spread the notion that the Cree nation was always here and so we owned the plains.

Reality reveals a very different picture.

In 1690, a teenager named Henry Kelsey was the first white man to see Saskatchewan. He had been sent down from York Factory by the Hudson's Bay Company accompanied by a group of Cree Indians. His job was to explore and convince the local Indians to go to York Factory to trade their furs.

For close to a century, the Hudson's Bay Company had done its trading on the shores of Hudson Bay at York Factory at the mouth of the York River. To keep them there, the Cree people who lived around the bay told them stories of fierce tribes and monsters that lived inland. This apparently scared off the company, allowing the Cree to take the trade goods and develop their own trading system inland.

Finally the company decided that they should find out what was happening inland. Expeditions were sent up the York River, into Lake Winnipeg, and finally up the Saskatchewan to Cumberland House.

Cumberland House was also known as Pine Island and was the highest and driest part of the delta area. It had been a traditional gathering and trading place for generations. From Cumberland House the fur traders could travel north on the Churchill or head south onto the plains by way of the Saskatchewan River.

Saskatchewan was settled from the top down. Saskatchewan's oldest church is the Anglican Church at Stanley Mission. It was built in 1856, long before there were comparable structures in the south.

The Saskatchewan River was the main corridor from the north to the south.

Henry Kelsey found a vast virgin plain and great herds of buffalo. He also encountered nations that today have been greatly dispersed. The Saskatchewan River formed the boundary between the various nations. The Dene lived to the north, the Gros Ventre and Assiniboine to the south, and further south and to the west was the Blackfoot confederacy, which consisted of the Blackfoot, Piegan, and Blood peoples.

Life on the plains was hard. The climate was harsh and there was little protection from the elements. Large wolf packs and the plains grizzly preyed on the great herds of buffalo. It was a dangerous place for human beings.

Kelsey's expedition was halted at the present site of the town of Nipawin when they were driven back by the Gros Ventre and Snake Indians (also known as the northern Shoshonee), who inhabited the northern plains. Sites like present-day Wanuskewin were most likely Gros Ventre camping places. The town of Leask and the Mistawasis reserve are located on the Snake Plains, named after the Snake Indians.

The Cree were forest people, and at first they were not welcome on the plains. Using trade goods such as rifles, they came up the Saskatchewan and settled on the plains, displacing other nations.

The fur trade flourished over the years and the Cree obtained firearms and ventured out on the plains. What followed throughout the 1700s and 1800s were years of conquest and war on the plains. The Gros Ventre and Snake Indians moved to present-day Montana, Idaho, and Washington State.

As the Cree moved south, they named their new land. *Saskatchewan* means swift flowing, an indication of the condition of the river upstream from its sluggish state in the Cumberland delta.

Squaw Rapids is really *Iskwew Pawistik,* which means woman rapids, probably because they were gentle and didn't require a portage where the women and children would have to walk while the men traversed the rapids. The pejorative name "squaw" is a derivation from the original Cree word *iskwew.*

Nipawin means a place where they stand and wait. Its location affords a long view of the river downstream. It was here where the people would wait and watch for their hunters or the fur traders. When the Nipawin hydroelectric dam was built, archaeological research was done on the affected area and numerous trading posts were discovered. The Saskatchewan River was a major trading centre, and it was fought over by the North West Company, the Hudson's Bay Company, and numerous free traders.

Further up river on the James Smith First Nation are several important sites, including Fort a la Corne, a North West Company trading post. It is the earliest recorded farming community in the province. The first Saskatchewan grain crop was planted there.

Also nearby is the historic site called Pihonanis, the little waiting place. Families would camp and wait here for the men to return from hunting and travelling up the river.

The Saskatchewan River valley is also rich in First Nations sites. Numerous camping places have been uncovered, including several large gathering places.

The Saskatchewan River from the forks to Cumberland House is an historic stretch of waterway that represents the transition from the forest to the plains. The northern people lived off the river and harvested fish, in contrast to southern nations, which ignored fishing.

The Saskatchewan River was the highway for generations of Indian people, the fur trade, and settlers' steamboats. Long before the railway was built, the Saskatchewan River was the gateway to the province.

A New Economy Built on Fur

The fur trade opened up the Northwest, but its effect on the way of life of the First Nations has been misrepresented. To say that Indians were routinely exploited and ripped off in the fur trade period is to sell them short.

The fur traders travelled thousands of kilometres into the heart of the Northwest. They had to get along with their suppliers. If they behaved badly or offered outrageously low prices for pelts, they had a long way to run for cover. They couldn't just call head office for support.

The fur traders became a part of the culture and were well known by the people and their leaders. I suppose there were traders who thought they could try and pull a fast one on their Native customers, but they didn't last. Reputation was everything and competition and communication dealt with the shysters.

The Hudson's Bay Company was operated from England by a group of aristocrats led by Prince Rupert. Now I'm pretty sure that Prince Rupert and his Company of Adventurers had no concerns about the effects of the fur trade on Canada's development. They never set foot in Canada and instead left it up to their minions to carry out the daily work. These factors and clerks were sent out to trading posts, where they were completely cut off from England for years at a time. They became part of the community. They learned the language, made friends and married into local families.

The fur trade may have been driven by a company of adventurers in England and businessmen from Montreal, but in the end it changed the face of the West forever. The first fur traders found a country that was both politically and physically far different from today. Their descendants live on in the Métis and First Nations. In the end, they didn't conquer as much as they simply blended in.

Horse and Gun – The Tools of a New Culture

With the fur trade, the First Nations moved onto the plains in greater numbers, and by combining trade goods such as firearms with the mobility of the horse, a new culture – the horse culture – was born.

When firearms from the fur traders were combined with the horse that had been introduced by the Spanish, the result was highly mobile and efficient hunters. Before the fur trade, the plains were sparsely inhabited by the Blackfoot, the Gros Ventre, and other peoples in the West such as the Kootenay.

The fur trade came from the east, and the horse from the south. The tribes that benefited came from those directions. The Sioux came out of Minnesota, the Cree from the north, the Saulteaux, also known as the Plains Ojibway, came from the northeast.

The Cree claimed the plains, and by 1850 their empire extended to Moose Mountain and the Cypress Hills in the south and the Churchill River in the north. Their empire extended across the northern part of present-day Alberta into northeastern British Columbia. Communities were created along the Peace River all the way to the eastern end of Lake Athabasca, to present-day Fort Chipewyan. The southern end of the Cree Empire in Alberta was at the Peace Hills and the site of the present-day town of Wetaskewin.

Other tribes such as the Blackfoot were forced westward and in some cases into the mountains.

The Cree were able to expand rapidly because of their alliance with the Saulteaux and Assiniboine nations. By becoming allies, they were able to drive the other tribes south and west and gain vast amounts of land in the process.

The plains became a battleground as tribes fought for land and expanded their territory. The last great battle was fought near Fort Whoop-up near the present-day city of Lethbridge.

Several bands of Cree attacked a Blackfoot camp. The Cree outnumbered the Blackfoot, but the Blackfoot had recently acquired repeating rifles. The result was carnage on both sides, and the Cree retreated in defeat.

This new technology proved to be so deadly that a peace treaty was made before both sides suffered too much. The Cree and Blackfoot nations gathered and agreed to live in peace and not fight each other. They agreed on the land that each nation would occupy. The treaty negotiations took place north of the Bear Hills. We know this place today as Wetaskewin. *Wetaskewin* means "place of peace" in Cree.

To cement the treaty, they conducted an exchange of children. Cree children went to live with the Blackfoot and Blackfoot children went to live with the Cree. This was the insurance policy that assured the success of the treaty.

The practice continued, and Poundmaker was raised by Chief Crowfoot in this manner. As a result, the two nations grew closer together and their languages and cultures intermingled.

It was a time of war and conquest, and the face of the plains was changed forever. The numbered treaties followed the treaty of Wetaskewin, and peace returned to the plains.

1885 and Beyond

When we look back on the settlement of the West, Indian people assisted the early settlers and formed important partnerships that have become obscured by time and myth.

Canadians like to assume that we are morally superior to the Americans. We play a peacekeeping role while our neighbours to the south are depicted as warmongers and bullies. And nowhere is this myth more apparent than in the history of the settling of the West and the treatment accorded the First Nations.

The mythology and misunderstanding about the Northwest Resistance and the role played by the First Nations continues in spite of the historical record that shows that the First Nations had their own agenda. In spite of the press accounts and public sentiment at the time, the First Nations had separate issues and remained loyal to the Crown.

First Nations people have long known that our past leaders had a separate agenda from the Métis, but history has recorded the uprisings and skirmishes of 1885 as massacres and a series of associated events. The reality is that the First Nations leaders honoured the treaties and were faced with an arrogant and uncaring government that forced the chain of events that finally led to the violence.

In the 1880s, Canada had already made treaty with the First Nations, and the influx of settlers had not yet begun. The country was still constructing the national railway, which ended somewhere in the Shield of northern Ontario.

The loss of the buffalo had a devastating effect on the First Nations and the Métis. The buffalo had been the backbone of the economy of the West. The federal government had failed to keep the treaty promises, and Indian people were suffering from starvation, disease, and deprivation.

In the spring of 1885, the West was a hotbed of discontent. The events that followed could have been predicted.

This situation was not helped by the colonial administrators that were sent out to control the Indians. Hayter Reed, the Indian agent in Battleford, was known as "Iron Heart" by the local Indians. Apparently, the name was apt and there was no love lost between them because he referred to the local Indians as "the scum of the plains."

Indian Affairs followed a policy of tight-fisted parsimony at a time when the Indian people were starving. Government rations consisted of salt pork, flour, and beans. This food may have been easy to preserve and store but it was a far cry from the fresh meat our people were used to. These rations were cut back and withheld at the will of the Indian agent.

The arrogant and racist attitude of the government officials was the primary cause of the Indian rebellion in the Northwest. But the government and press of the day deliberately wrapped all the issues into one to instil a sense of panic and mindless nationalism in eastern Canadians. If one believed the press reports of the day, the whole West was aflame.

This was necessary to entice volunteers to come out and fight the rebels. The government had to mobilize to put down what it portrayed as an Indian-Métis insurrection. This was also the time of the Indian Wars in the United States, and the press was rife with biased reports from the "front."

The military leaders of the day were British colonial officers who held local people in contempt and were anxious to plant the British flag on every part of the globe. Canada may have become a newly independent nation, but the old vestiges of the British Empire lingered on.

The Saskatchewan chiefs, meanwhile, had been meeting with government officials to try and get some action on the promises in the treaties.

Poundmaker led a delegation of other chiefs and leaders to Battleford to meet with the officials. The delegation wanted assistance for their people following a winter of famine and extreme hardship. But when he got to Battleford, all the officials and townspeople were hiding in the fort and refused to speak to the delegation.

The warriors were enraged, and the chiefs could no longer

control them. They proceeded to loot the town and take the food that their families so badly needed. Today, this action is referred to as the siege of Battleford. Indians refer to it as the time they looted the town. This action was the justification Colonel Otter needed to attack the sleeping camp at Cut Knife Hill.

The Battle at Cut Knife Hill is a part of our history that historians reluctantly refer to as a minor victory for the Indians but is seen by the First Nations as a clear victory.

Colonel Otter headed out to Poundmaker's reserve with the idea that he was going to teach the Indians a good lesson. Although they attacked in the predawn, they were defeated. Otter's troops retreated in disarray. The Indian warriors had taken on a superior-equipped force and beaten them.

But in the end, the government prevailed, and leaders like Poundmaker, who was a man of peace, were treated like traitors and sentenced to Stony Mountain Penitentiary. There was no understanding of First Nations government; there was no attempt to heal the wounds of the past. Instead, officials like Hayter Reed called for complete repression, total disarmament, and revenge. This would set the stage for government policy for years to come.

It was after the resistance that the full force of the system was brought to bear on the leaders and their people. First, all the leaders were rounded up and tried. Much is made of the trial of Louis Riel, but the trials of Big Bear and others were kangaroo courts in comparison.

A total of some forty-five "rebels" were sent to Stony Mountain Penitentiary outside Winnipeg. The number sentenced was more than the penitentiary could house. A new wing had to be built to accommodate them.

Eight of the "rebels" were sentenced to death. The eight were hung at Fort Battleford in what is the largest public hanging in

Canadian history. The Indian children at the Battleford Industrial School were forced to witness the hanging. People were also brought in from the nearby Moosomin and Thunderchild reserves. The message was clear. This is what we're capable of, so know your place.

The eight are buried in a mass grave located just down the hill from the provincial campground in Battleford.

One of the rebels sentenced to the penitentiary was my great-grandfather, Misatimwas. He was the warrior leader under Chief Little Pine. His duty was to protect the camp when the militia attacked at the Battle of Cut Knife Hill. When the army attacked at dawn, he mounted a horse and organized the defences. The warriors set up a defensive position under the leadership of Poundmaker's warrior chief, Fine Day.

Misatimwas was shot through the abdomen while protecting the women and children. He survived his wounds and spent three years in Stony Mountain.

Big Bear was sentenced to three years but was released after a year. He travelled to the Little Pine reserve, where he died a broken, heartsick old man. Poundmaker was released after a year and a half suffering from tuberculosis. He travelled to Blackfoot Crossing to be with his adoptive father, Chief Crowfoot. Poundmaker died on the Blackfoot reserve in 1887.

Other chiefs died in prison or shortly after. Chief One Arrow died in prison and is buried at the bishop's residence in Winnipeg.

The revenge on the part of the Canadian government was swift and cruel. All the horses, firearms, and weapons were confiscated. Anything that could be used as a weapon was taken, including knives, hatchets, and so on.

Many of the people fled to the United States. Much is made about Sitting Bull seeking the protection of the Crown after the

Battle of the Little Big Horn, but the flight of Canadian Indians to the United States is ignored.

It is part of Canadian folklore that in 1876 Sitting Bull sought sanctuary in Canada following the Battle at the Little Big Horn. Sitting Bull stated that he came to Canada seeking the protection of the Queen from the Americans who were bent on revenge. Sitting Bull was granted asylum because Canada wanted to assert its sovereignty over the West and also because it had no military force to handle him and his people.

But there is another story. Following the Northwest Resistance, Canadian Indian people, especially the Cree and Assiniboine, headed south and sought sanctuary in the United States from the revengeful reprisals of the Canadian government.

My grandfather, Josie Cuthand, and his mother joined the exodus to the south. My great-grandmother died during the trek. The details are sketchy but it is felt that she fell victim to disease.

When Misatimwas returned to the reserve, he was considered the chief by his people. But, since he was considered to be a "rebel" by the government, his position was not recognized by the Department of Indian Affairs. This was common practice by the government as they sought to weed out the troublemakers and establish a more compliant leadership.

My grandfather lived in the States for close to fifteen years. During this period he worked for the US Army at Fort Assiniboine in Montana and danced in a Wild West Show. He travelled throughout the northern states and made it as far as Chicago.

In one of the large cities he met an Indian from the eastern states who told him what to expect when the white people came to settle their land. He told him that their future lay in education. My grandfather remembered this and made sure that in the future his children got a good education.

He travelled around the United States by riding the rails. At that time, Bannock Indians, a tribe from Oregon who were members of the Northern Paiute, could ride free on the railcar couplings. He wrapped himself up in a blanket and wore a black hat in the style of the Bannock Indians. Eventually, he returned, and lived within the expatriate group in Montana.

Some of the Canadian Indians lived just across the border in Fort Assiniboine; others travelled as far away as Flathead Lake; but most settled around Great Falls, forming a large encampment on the east side of the city. According to accounts at the time, the east side of Great Falls was one large Indian slum.

Around the turn of the century, the American government decided to round up all the "strays and stragglers" and send them home. Some reservation land was set aside for some of the refugees. Today, this is known as the Rocky Boy reservation, the only Cree reservation in the United States.

Under the leadership of Big Bear's son, Little Bad Man or Ayimisis, some of the Cree were able to settle on the newly created Rocky Boy reservation. Ayimisis and his people lobbied hard for a home reservation in the United States because they knew that they would have no home in Canada. Northern Montana had been Cree hunting territory and the border was considered only of minor importance.

Others intermarried with local tribes, particularly the Crow. Today, Cree people from Canada still keep in touch with their relatives in Montana.

Others were not treated as well. Since they had no US citizenship and no recognizable leader, the US government regarded the rest as "strays" and therefore they were to be shipped out of the country. My grandfather was one of the deportees. In 1898, a large number of Cree were assembled and marched to the border.

What happened at the border was a typical example of the way Canada and the United States handled the administration of the West and its original inhabitants. A large number of US Cavalry escorted the ragtag group to the forty-ninth parallel. Some had horses, others had teams and wagons, others simply walked. At the border, they received a stern warning to never come back and were turned over to the local authorities. The local authorities, as it turned out, were two members of the North-West Mounted Police.

Everyone waited patiently while they sorted things out. Those with home reserves to go to were sent on their way. Those who were not members of a band were sent up to the Bear Hills, where a reserve had been surveyed for them. This reserve is known today as the Montana Band.

One of the constables then escorted my grandfather and several other Cree to their reserves in the Battleford area. The constable's name was Daniel Davis. My grandfather knew him as "Peach." According to Bill McKay at the RCMP museum in Regina, he received his nickname because of his love of peaches. He was only twenty-three years old but spoke Cree and was familiar with and sympathetic to Indian culture. He was described in a report as "a sinewy, weather-beaten and hardy constable of good reputation."

The report describes the epic journey. The group was quite large and consisted of Chiefs Grizzly Bear's Head, Poor Man, and Thunderchild. The group travelled north, and within eighteen days they arrived at Battleford. Poor Man had apparently left earlier and settled on his reserve in the Touchwood Hills.

Grizzly Bear's Head settled on reserve land next to Red Pheasant in the Eagle Hills south of Battleford. Thunderchild moved onto his reserve east of Battleford, on the site of the present-day town of Delmas. My grandfather travelled west to the Little Pine reserve and joined the rest of his family.

The history of the Canadian West is anything but dull.

Profile – Shanawdithit

Two historical individuals are the subject of jubilation and mourning in Newfoundland. Giovanni Coboto and Shanawdithit, individuals largely unknown to Canadians, represent both the pride and shame of two nations.

Giovanni Coboto was an Italian navigator who was retained by the British in 1496 to find a route to the Orient. Four years earlier, another Italian, Christopher Columbus, had been retained by Spain for the same reason and had discovered the West Indies. (The Italians, it seems, were good at hiring themselves out but never established an empire of their own. If they had, the Americas would have been one big Italian-speaking colony and we would be all driving Fiats. But I digress.)

In school we were told that a guy named John Cabot discovered Newfoundland. This was the British way of leaving the impression that an Englishman had made the first voyage to North America.

They say history is written by the conquerors and it would seem that our history is no different. The Vikings were in North America about five hundred years before the voyage of Cabot. Of course, the First Nations were here long before. The British "discovered" what had really existed for centuries.

Which brings us to Shanawdithit, the last known member of the Beotuk nation. When she and her aunt Demasduwit were captured in 1823, there were only an estimated thirteen members of the Beotuk nation alive in the interior of Newfoundland.

Both woman developed tuberculosis, and Demasduwit soon died. Shanawdithit lived on until 1829. When she died, the Beotuk nation died with her.

The Beotuks were victims of European diseases, particularly tuberculosis. They were also regarded as vermin by the settlers and forced farther and farther into the interior. They were cut off from their traditional food source, the sea, and they had to exist on the limited resources of the interior.

The Beotuks had been a proud ocean-going people that hunted on the bird islands off the coast and fished in the rich coastal waters. When they were forced inland, their beautiful canoes were restricted to lakes and brooks. They fell victim to malnutrition and disease.

The Beotuk had always avoided European contact, and the only way they could be studied was to be captured alive. After Shanawdithit was captured, she provided the only eyewitness account of her people's last twenty years, an account that she could never narrate without tears.

Following her death, Beotuk graves were robbed for museums, and the only record of these peaceful people exists in museum storage vaults.

It is doubtful that Giovanni Caboto ever laid eyes on the Beotuk, but following groups of fishermen, settlers, and trappers would infect the island with European diseases that eventually led to the end of a beautiful people.

This is the story of the "conquest" of the New World. The Europeans unknowingly conquered the Americas by germ warfare. Whole families, villages, tribes, and nations were wiped out by the epidemics that swept across the continent. Far more First Nations people perished because of epidemics than through warfare with the European conquerors.

Profile – Sweetgrass

Today's reserves are named after the original chiefs that signed the treaties, men like Red Pheasant, Beardy, Thunderchild, Piapot, and White Bear.

If you travel west of Battleford, you will come across the Sweetgrass First Nation. This reserve is named after one of the Cree's leading negotiators and spokesman when Treaty Number Six was signed at Fort Pitt in 1876.

It's ironic that one of our leading historical figures represented the Cree nation but was not born a Cree.

Many years earlier, the Cree were at war with the Pawistikwiyiniwak, or the Little Rapid People. These people lived along the South Saskatchewan River and were known to the French fur traders as the Gros Ventre. As was the custom back then, only warriors engaged in war, and women and children were not harmed. During one skirmish, however, the Cree captured a young boy and took him back to their camp.

A widow rushed up and told the warriors that the boy looked like her lost son and she wanted to raise him as her own child. She was given the boy, who became known as Okimasis, which means Little Chief and He-who-has-no-name.

He remained small when he grew up and was the subject of taunts and derision from the warriors, who didn't consider him worthy. One day he told his mother that since they were poor he would have to leave the camp and steal horses from the Blackfoot. His mother made him a new pair of moccasins and he made rope.

He travelled alone, walking and running to the south country. He travelled at night, sleeping during the day. Early one morning he came upon a narrow valley that was filled with fog. He looked closer and saw tipi poles poking out of the fog, and a short distance away he saw a herd of horses.

He crept forward and went toward the herd. He hid in the bushes, and a man approached. He crept closer and shot the man using his bow and arrow. The man hit the ground without uttering a sound. Okimasis crept out of the bushes and took the dead man's gun and then scalped him. He then caught a fine bay stallion by its trailing rope and drove off the entire herd. The Blackfoot were left with only a few stray horses, and they were unable to catch up with him.

Several days later he returned to his camp with forty-two ponies. He gave his mother five and told her to gather up the poor people who had few horses. He gave away the remaining horses and kept the bay stallion for himself.

Later that day, an old man came back to the camp. He had been away when the horses were given out. When he asked if there was a horse for him, the young man gave him the bay stallion. He also gave him the scalp he had taken from the fallen Blackfoot. The old man was deeply touched and told him he would give him the name Kind Sweetgrass Person. He also told him that, because of his kindness and bravery, someday he would be chief.

By 1870, he was the principal chief of a large area of the central plains area in what would become Saskatchewan and Alberta. That year he confessed to Father Lacombe that he had become a chief by killing a man and stealing horses. All his life since, he had been haunted by the death of the man because he had shot him while the man was saying his prayers. Later, Sweetgrass was baptized a Christian and took the name Abraham.

By 1870, events beyond their control had begun to affect the Cree nation. The government of Canada purchased Rupert's Land from the Hudson's Bay Company in anticipation of the building of a national railroad. The United States was looking northward to expand into Canada, and American whiskey traders were creating havoc in the southern plains. Coupled with this, the ravages of disease and the loss of the great herds of buffalo meant the life of the First Nations of the plains was about to change forever.

The Canadian government sent out emissaries to make treaty with the First Nations. In 1876, they concluded Treaty Number Six at Fort Carlton and Fort Pitt.

Sweetgrass was one of the leading spokesmen. He spoke positively about the treaty. By now he was a respected elder and his word was valued by both sides. When the chiefs signed the treaty, they received presents from the queen, including a suit of clothes, a treaty medal, and a beautiful gun. They also received a flag that they were to fly over their lodge, recognizing their authority and the fact that Canada now owned the West.

When Sweetgrass returned to his home in the Frog Lake area, he was confronted by some of his people who felt that the deal was too harsh and he had given away too much. His brother-in-law took the gun Sweetgrass had received for signing the treaty and shot him.

Later the band would move to their land west of Battleford, but the name of their reserve would be called Sweetgrass after their chief, who died for doing what he thought was right for his adopted people.

CHAPTER THREE

THE POWER
OF WORDS

The exploration of North America reflects competing empires, fur traders, and adventurers looking for a shortcut to the Orient. The role played by the First Nations is both obvious and forgotten, but their contribution to that exploration can still be seen in the place names of this continent.

Modern Names Reflect the Past

The Europeans who explored the new land were either lost and alone or being guided by the First Nations. Canada is built on the existing trade routes and landmarks of the First Nations. The explorers followed the rivers and trails that had formed the highways for centuries.

The Americas never needed to be discovered. They were opened up to European contact. Explorers basically followed the existing trails and trade routes. If they wanted to know where they were, they simply asked the local inhabitants.

Jacques Cartier landed in the New World, planted the French flag, erected a cross, and claimed the land in the name of the French king, much to the amusement of the local Mi'kmaq.

He asked them where he was and they told him "Gaspeg" or "the place where the land ends."

He went further up the river to a place where it narrowed. He again asked the locals where he was and they told him "Kebec," which is Algonquin for "where the river narrows."

It seems that a lot of places are named because the explorers were lost and needed to know the name of a particular place.

The French renamed landmarks using saints' names, as did the Spanish. The British used names from the Royal family until they ran out: Victoria, Prince Albert, Prince Rupert, Prince George, Queen Charlotte, and so on. However, sometimes a First Nations name would be used.

Canada is an Iroquois word meaning a cabin or lodge. *Ontario* takes its name from the lake and means beautiful sparkling water.

Some words are obviously Aboriginal in origin. *Chicago* means wild onion in Algonquin. *Winnipeg* means dirty water in Cree, *Ponoka* in Alberta is Cree for a black elk, and *Ottawa* is

Algonquin for trading place. Some landmarks are more descriptive, such as *Tadoussac* in Quebec, which means breasts, referring to the rounded mountains at the mouth of the Saguenay River.

Saskatchewan too has many landmarks that were famous long before the land was settled by the newcomers.

The Saskatchewan River system cuts across the prairies, and for centuries it has been a major landmark. It was an important source of water in a dry land. *Saskatchewan* means fast-flowing water in Cree. The South Saskatchewan River is called the Elk or Red Deer River in Cree. The name comes from the Red Deer River that joins the Saskatchewan River. The original inhabitants tracked the river from the northwest, and each river that joined it became a part of the river. The rivers that join the Red Deer are the Bow, the Old Man, the Waterton, and the Belly, among others. The Belly River got its name because, when, a rider forded it, the water came up to the belly of the horse. It wasn't very imaginative, but it was descriptive.

The Saskatchewan or Elk River is a rich chain of First Nations landmarks and history.

To the south of Saskatoon where Diefenbaker Lake now sits was the great rock Misstussini. This was a Native gathering place and source of spiritual strength for centuries.

Many years ago when the world was young there was a small group of people travelling across the prairie. They were using travois pulled by dogs. Among these people there was an old lady with a big dog pulling a big travois, and in the travois was a little boy.

They came to a place where there were a lot of buffalo, and as they came close the dogs chased the buffalo and stampeded them. The big dog ran off, and the old lady couldn't stop it. The leash slipped out of her hands and away went the dog with the boy in the travois.

They searched for a long time, but they never found the boy.

Meanwhile on the prairie were two buffalo bulls who lived by themselves. They were bachelors. Younger, stronger bulls had chased out the old bulls and taken over their harems. The two bulls were grazing quietly when they heard a young child crying. They paid no attention to it, but after a while the older bull said, "I think we should do something about this child crying and crying for a long time."

The younger bull said, "Oh no. The people are always chasing us, killing us. Let's just leave it alone. Let it be."

The old bull said, "I think we should go save the boy."

"No," said the younger bull. "I'll kill it when I get there."

The old bull said, "Let's have a race. If I get there first, we'll raise the child. If you get there first, you can do what you like."

So the two bulls started to run. The younger bull stumbled and so the old bull got there first. There was the child, sitting in the travois, with the dog missing.

So the old bull said, "Now we will look after this child." So they looked after the boy, and they took him to berry patches where he could eat. The boy grew to be a very handsome young man.

One day the old bull, Kind Old Man Buffalo, said, "We are now going to where the sun sets, where there is a big meeting. Everybody will be there. But you are not one of us and you will have to stay away from the crowd. These bulls are very mean, very jealous, they fight each other, and if you make a mistake, if you even talk to one of the women, they'll kill you."

So they travelled for days, and they came to a place with a wide plain near a river. There were a lot of buffalo. Kind Old Man Buffalo said, "Now you have to stay here while we go. Be sure not to go anywhere, and don't talk to anybody." So the young man sat on a flat rock and stayed there, and the old bulls went with the crowd. What they were celebrating we don't know.

Later the young man had a vision. There was a beautiful young woman coming down to the pool. She was dressed all in buckskin. The young man jumped off the flat rock and ran down and asked her for some water to drink.

"Oh, come here," she said. She took a shell and gave it to him. He drank and drank. She filled her bag to take home. The young man ran up to the rock, and sat there. As soon as the young woman filled her bag, she started to yell, "Heyyy! That Kind Old Man Buffalo's son touched me."

Everybody heard it, so Kind Old Man Buffalo came running back, and he said, "Now you are in trouble. That beautiful woman you saw was one of the white bull's wives. He is very jealous, he is very powerful, and he is one of the largest bulls around here. He is the chief buffalo. Now he wants to kill you. He will meet you, and you have to fight."

So the next day all the buffalo stood in a great big circle and Kind Old Man Buffalo took his son there. He said, "You are not one of us, and you cannot fight the bull. I want you to roar four times to Kewatin, the North Wind." And so the boy did. And he said, "I want you to roar four times towards Wapun, the East Wind." And the boy did. And he said, "Now roar four times to Sawin, the South Wind." The boy did. Then he said, "Now roar four times towards the setting sun, Nepawanuk," as they called the West Wind. And when the boy had roared four times, he transformed into a beautiful buffalo. He stood up. "Now you are one of us," said Kind Old Man Buffalo, "Now you have to fight the Great White Buffalo. He is coming."

The Great White Buffalo's feet were digging into the earth, he was so big and strong. Kind Old Man Buffalo said, "You have to be careful. He is tricky. Face him all the time. The only weakness he has is behind his front legs. If you can gore him, you can kill him. He is very quick, but you are young, you are quick."

The Great White Buffalo came with his head down, and he said, "So you would touch my wife. I'm going to walk around you four times and then I am going to charge."

Kind Old Man Buffalo yelled at his son, "Be careful, face him, face him! Do what you can."

The Great White Buffalo charged after the fourth round, and they locked horns. He pushed the young bull back. The young bull pushed him back. They fought all day. And sometimes they would not be able to push each other; their front legs would lift up. They trembled with strength.

Finally, towards evening, Kind Old Man Buffalo yelled at his son, "Do what I say, try and throw him off balance." They were very tired. Sometimes they would stop, panting. Then they would charge again, and they trembled with strength, pushing each other. The young bull pushed, and twisted him. Suddenly, he gored him behind the front leg.

The white bull said, "You got me, you got me. Which way should I fall?"

The young bull said, "You can fall whichever way you want to."

"I'll fall towards Sawin, the South Wind," the Great White Buffalo said. And he fell, head down, and died.

The crowd moaned, and the bulls started to paw the ground. They were angry.

Kind Old Man Buffalo and his friend came running, and they said, "Now you have to go away. You cannot stay here, you are not one of us, and you can't go back to your people because you don't know them. They've been looking for you. Some day they will find you."

"Now I want you to roll four times towards Kewatin." And the boy did. "Now, towards Wapun." And he did. "Now roll four times towards Sawin, the South Wind." Again he did. "Now roll four times towards Nepawanuk, the West Wind." He did, and he transformed back into a handsome young man.

The two bulls walked on each side of him towards the setting sun. They walked for days, and in time they reached a beautiful place on the plain. Kind Old Man Buffalo said, "You can't go back to your people and you cannot stay with us. You have to become something else so you will be remembered for what you have done. People will come and they will celebrate and they will remember you."

"Now roll four times toward the North Wind, Kewatin, four times towards the East Wind, Wapun, four times towards the South Wind, Sawin, now four times towards Nepawanuk, the West Wind." The boy transformed into a mighty buffalo. Kind Old Man Buffalo prayed over him, stretching his hand along his back. And they left him.

One day, the Old Lady asked the medicine men if they could do something to find this young man. So they made the shaking tent, calling the spirits. "What happened to this boy that was lost?" they prayed.

Suddenly a spirit said, "He was discovered by the two bulls. They raised him, he became a handsome young man, he fought the white bull and overcame him, and he was changed into a rock as a remembrance for his great deed. You will find him, you will feel him, you'll go west towards the setting sun."

So they went, and the medicine man said, "I know we're pretty close to him." They saw a buffalo sitting on a prairie. It was a big rock. And they stayed there, they gave him gifts, they had a feast. And every year they went back to remember the great thing that he had done.

Years later, new people would come and live on the plains. They built a huge dam on the South Saskatchewan River that flooded the valley, including the great rock known as Mistassini. They tried to move it, but they broke it to pieces in the process. With it went one of our great spiritual gathering places. It remains alive in our people's hearts and minds today.

Cities Have Roots in Aboriginal Settlements

Further west on the river is the city of Medicine Hat. The origins of this place are part of First Nations history, and fortunately the name wasn't changed when the railway went through. One of the great mistakes when the West was opened up for settlement was that place names often came from a CPR list in Toronto or Montreal instead of from the country itself. Prairie towns were named for surveyors, wives of railway barons, and other individuals.

Medicine Hat stands out as a survivor from an earlier time. The story of Medicine Hat was told to me by my father, who learned of it from his father.

At one time, there was a small band of Blackfoot living in the foothills of the Rocky Mountains. Their chief was an old man who had several wives. His youngest wife grew bored with the tedious existence of a young woman married to an old man. But her husband had a young brother. Soon romance blossomed, and they decided to run away together. This was a risky decision since the chief could hunt them down and kill them both, but they decided to tempt fate and take the chance.

Their plan was to leave at night, but before they left they had to gather their possessions. For several days they met in the woods near the camp and hid the things they would take on their journey. Then one night they met and slipped away.

They decided to head east into Cree country in the hope that their people would look for them in the mountains. The plan worked: their people searched the mountain valleys.

The young couple travelled east along the great river that cut across the prairies through what would someday be southern Alberta. They found a secluded place beside the river near a high cutbank. It was here that the young couple pitched their lodge and set up housekeeping.

For some time they remained there undiscovered, but because they were now in the land of the Cree they always had to be on their guard. They were camped inside a bluff of trees, cooking fires had to be small, and they constantly scanned the prairie for signs of bands of Cree warriors.

One day, they spotted a man heading along the river in the direction of the camp. He was by himself, but he had a string of pack horses that were carrying trade goods, buffalo hides, and other furs. He was shorter than a Blackfoot, and he wore a tall black hat. Clearly this was an enemy, and if he found them he would kill them both.

The young man climbed to the top of the cutbank, and when the stranger passed underneath he jumped on him and plunged his knife deep into the man's chest. The man fell to the ground dead. When he fell, his tall hat fell off, revealing that it was full of medicine.

The couple checked the spoils of the attack and made a horrible discovery: The man was part of a raiding party, and some of the booty came from their home camp.

The couple broke camp and headed west to see what remained of their families and friends. When they arrived, they found that most of the people had survived the attack, but the old chief had been among those killed.

The young man returned the stolen loot, but he kept the hat

with all the medicine. His people heralded him as a hero. Later, they would choose him to be their chief, and he and his young wife lived together in harmony and prosperity.

The place of the attack would forever be known as Medicine Hat. Today, different people live there, but the history lives on in the name.

N ames for cities on the prairies come from a variety of sources. This is because the West is very young in historic terms. As First Nations people, we can talk to elders who watched the cities grow and know them in ways we can only imagine.

I recall once speaking to an elder from the Enoch First Nation west of Edmonton who remembered hunting rabbits where Jasper Avenue now runs. Some cities' names are purely artificial, while others coincide with First Nations gathering places. One in particular was founded by the First Nations.

Regina, Lloydminster, and Moose Jaw are examples of cities that were founded by settlers and land speculators. The capital of the North-West Territories was originally established at Battleford, but when it was bypassed by the Canadian Pacific Railway, the government decided to move the capital south. One possible site was Fort Qu'Appelle, but speculators bought up the land around the fort, so the CPR and Lieutenant Governor Dewdney decided to establish a city in the middle of the plains at Wascana Creek so they could profit from the land sales.

Saskatoon, on the other hand, was created as a temperance colony, but archaeological evidence has shown that the down-town area and the Wanuskewin valley were First Nations gathering places for millennia. It is a case of both peoples discovering a good thing.

Battleford too was a long-time crossroads for Aboriginal people. At this point, where the Battle River joins the North Saskatchewan, the river could be safely forded. The North Saskatchewan River runs swift and deep on both sides of this point, so it was a valuable and strategic location. The Battle River, or "fighting river," was named because, at one time, it formed the boundary between the warring Blackfoot and Cree nations.

But Prince Albert stands out as a city that was truly founded by Aboriginal people. Originally known as *Kestapinik* in Cree, it was a gathering and trading place for the Cree and Dene peoples. In 1776, Peter Pond established a trading post near the present-day site of Prince Albert. Later, the North West Company established a trading post on the same site. In 1821, when the Hudson's Bay Company merged with the North West Company, the post reverted to the HBC.

The first family to settle in the area was the "Scots halfbreed" family of James and Margaret Isbister. James Isbister was the clerk at the Hudson's Bay Company trading post at Fort a la Corne in the 1850s.

Fort a la Corne is located today on the James Smith First Nation. It was named after Captain Louis, Chevalier de La Corne, a member of the North West Company who established a string of posts beyond Lake Superior.

James Isbister was the son of John Isbister, who was born in the Orkney Isles. The Hudson's Bay Company preferred Orkney Islanders because they were industrious men who were used to harsh weather. They also adapted well. They married local women and their offspring formed the basis of the Scots Métis, whose descendants are found in Indian and Métis communities throughout western Canada. John Isbister married Fanny Sinclair, a woman of Orkney – Native parentage. James

Isbister married Margaret Bear, the daughter of William Bear, who lived in the Carlton area.

James and Margaret set up housekeeping in 1862 east of what is now the Saskatchewan Penitentiary. Later they farmed further east near the present-day Muskoday reserve. Bear is now a common family name on the Muskoday reserve, and the roots quite possibly come from William Bear and his family.

In 1866, the first group of settlers arrived at Kestapinik. They were a group of Scots Métis. The only white man in the group was a Presbyterian minister, James Nisbet.

A community soon developed; it was known as Nisbit Mission. The log church that they built still stands in the city's Bryant Park. The settlement prospered, and by 1874 there were 288 persons living in the vicinity of the mission.

The land had been surveyed in river lots. In 1878, Dominion land surveyors arrived and tried to survey the land following north – south meridian lines. This caused a number of complaints, but they were ignored by the government.

In 1884, James Isbister accompanied Gabriel Dumont to Montana, where they convinced Louis Riel to return to Canada to speak for the Métis. Isbister took his grandson, Alex Fiddler, with him. Dumont was accompanied by Michael Dumas and Moise Ouellette.

Isbister was one of many who supported Riel until the movement broke into violent rebellion. During the rebellion, the Scots Métis remained neutral, and Prince Albert became an evacuation point for settlers fleeing from the violence in the south.

In 1866, the Reverend James Nisbit renamed the mission Prince Albert after the prince consort to Queen Victoria, who had died in 1861. Kestapinik is now a forgotten name, but it was the roots of this province's truly Aboriginal city.

Aboriginal Words Enrich Our Language

There is a story that John Diefenbaker used to tell of a young man who was immigrating to Canada and travelling across the prairies by train.

The train pulled into a station, and he got up to stretch his legs. He asked a local the name of the place and the reply was, "Saskatoon, Saskatchewan." A little later he came back to his seat and his travelling companion asked him where they were.

"I don't know," he replied. "They don't speak English."

Over the years, the English language has benefited from First Nations words, more than you may realize.

For example, a moose is a moose in both Cree and English. A *waskesiu* is an elk or red deer, but it is also the name for the townsite in Prince Albert National Park.

Moccasin is a word derived from the Cree word for footwear, *musksina*. The canoe is a First Nations invention and its name comes from the Algonquin language. Other Aboriginal inventions include the kayak, snowshoes, and the tipi.

Canada's national sport is not hockey but lacrosse, a game that was invented by the Iroquois. According to my father-in-law, who is Mohawk, the word *hockey* comes from the Mohawk language. One of the early explorers, possibly Champlain, was watching a game of lacrosse. He asked one of the locals what the game was called. Before he could reply one of the players was hit by the ball and yelled out "Agee!" which is Mohawk for "ouch." Thus the word hockey was invented. I don't know if this is true or not but it makes a good story.

When I was a kid up at La Ronge we used to go fishing on Sucker Lake. Later it was discovered by the tourists and the name was changed to the Woodland Cree equivalent, Nemeiben Lake. There was no cachet in a lake named Sucker but Nemeiben gave it an exotic feel. Namekus Lake in Prince Albert National Park also means sucker but in a southern Cree dialect.

Pipestone Lake was changed to Wapawekka Lake for the same reason. *Wapawekka* refers to the white sand hills and beaches that are special to the lake.

The Churchill River is called *Missinipi* in Cree, which means big water, referring to the chain of lakes that make up the Churchill River system. *Mississippi* means big river in both Ojibway and Cree. Since the river was discovered by fur traders from the north, it figures that it would have a Cree or Ojibway name. Apparently our ancestors didn't have much imagination when it came to naming rivers because *Yukon* means big river in the Athapaskan language as well. *Missoula* means feared water, *Missouri* means muddy water, and *Mississauga* means a river with many outlets.

Indian Names

I went to an integrated high school and I remember how the white kids would snicker and make fun of our last names. "Whatcha do, cut your hand? Ha Ha!" They tried to make us feel ashamed, and it was one more thing that separated us from them.

My last name is my grandfather's, and I have always carried it with pride.

But what about European names, the names of the kids who thought they were so cool? They're hardly as imaginative as Aboriginal names. Smith refers to a blacksmith, Cooper was a man who made barrels, and Clark was a paper pusher. Johnson was the son of John, Carlson was the son of Carl, and so on. This is hardly the stuff of a fertile imagination.

Aboriginal names can tell the story of people's lives. They identify people by their personal preferences, where they came from, and what spirits protected them. And they are unique. A name can serve as an Aboriginal postal code indicating which First Nation the individual calls home.

When the reserve system was put in place, a census was taken; the names were recorded and not changed. Today's last names are a snapshot of the band lists frozen in the late 1800s. Under the new system, women were obliged to take the name of their husband, and the family names we see today are male names only. The beautiful names that were given to women are a thing of the past.

In British Columbia, they paid the highest price. The West Coast languages were too hard for English ears to understand, and they didn't bother to try. They used the first names for the last and the result is family names such as George, Paul, Bob, Sam, and Jack. An entire heritage was wiped out because the colonial masters failed to understand a language and respect a people's heritage.

Indian people on the plains could be given a number of names throughout their life. The first was a baby name, the second was given when the person grew up, the third was a name for a family person, and the final name was given to an elder. These names had to be earned, and some would never achieve elder status or earn the name.

Today's baby names include families such as Newborn, Lone Child, and Born with a Tooth. Cuthand is my grandfather's baby name and refers to the results of frostbite to his hands when he was a baby.

Warrior names were based on acts of bravery and valour. For many years the head chief of the Blood nation in Alberta was Chief Jim Shot on Both Sides. His name turned heads, and people thought it was funny. The story is much different. The original holder of the name was a Blackfoot warrior who was riding through a coulee when he was attacked on both sides by Crees. He galloped forward and the Cree shot at him from both sides of the coulee. They wanted his horse so they aimed at him, but through skilful riding and luck (and maybe a little bad shooting on the part of the Cree) he managed to get away. When he told his story, he was honoured to receive the name "He who was shot at on both sides."

Other names refer to a particular event in a person's life. One man sold a horse to a Frenchman. The horse was a fine looking animal but it had a form of epilepsy and every so often it would collapse in a faint. As a result, the seller was given the name "French Cheater." When it was recorded by an Indian agent, it was written down as Frencheater, which makes no sense.

A chief had the name "The Unfortunate Man" or *Kawacatoose* because of the death and tragedy in his family. When it was translated into English, it became Poorman, a name that has a completely different meaning. Unfortunately, the name was also given to his reserve until the First Nation reverted to the Cree name.

Other names referred to the family's clan or spirit protector, such as Eagle, Bear, Buffalo, Wolverine, and Kingfisher. The eagle is especially honoured, and this is reflected in names such as Strong Eagle and Big Eagle.

Some names described the individual's achievements or personal preferences, like Cattleman, Night Traveller, Many Grey Horses, Moose Hunter, Gambler, Many Wounds, and Poundmaker.

And still others are pure poetry. Names such as Mountain Horse, Eagle Speaker, Lone Thunder, and White Hawk paint beautiful images.

Indian names are now heard in all walks of life. A lawyer with the last name Opekokew may defend a client in a court of law.

Dr. Tootoosis is on call at the Royal University Hospital, Dr. Stonechild is a university professor, and some guy named Cuthand gets a byline in a daily newspaper.

Our names are an important part of our First Nations heritage, and we should know the story behind them and be proud. No matter where we move or what we do, we will continue to carry the names of our ancestors with us.

Aboriginal Languages Under Attack

While we are moving forward with more confidence and promise than in the past, our people are still facing some serious threats. The most serious threat lies in the future of our languages. It is not hyperbole to say that Aboriginal languages are under attack like no time in our history. We are facing the extinction of an important part of our distinct culture, and the losses are increasing at an alarming rate.

A report from Statistics Canada points out that, today, only four out of the fifty-two Aboriginal languages in Canada are considered secure from the threat of extinction: Cree, Dene, Inuktitut, and Ojibway. In Saskatchewan, we have both Cree and Saulteaux peoples. On the plains, the Saulteaux are members of the Ojibway nation. Both Cree and Ojibway are part of the Algonquian language group.

The key for the survival of a language is its "viability" or its chances of being passed to the next generation. For this to happen, the language must be spoken in the home and used in daily conversation. When English takes over, the Aboriginal language is submerged and fails to be passed along.

In the last century, about ten Aboriginal languages became extinct. Today, about a dozen are close to extinction. In some cases the language is retained by a small group of elders. For example, the Kutenai language has only 120 speakers remaining, and there are only 145 Tlingit speakers left alive.

This is a tragic situation for the First Nations. Our languages took centuries to develop, and now they may disappear in a few generations. The report from Statistics Canada indicates that the number of Aboriginal people whose language spoken at home is their Aboriginal language declined from 76 percent in 1981 to 65 percent in 1996. The average age of a person with an Aboriginal mother tongue went up from age twenty-eight in 1981 to thirty-one in 1996.

The loss of a language is a major blow to a culture. In many cases the culture ceases to exist. The oral history in the mother tongue disappears, the grandparents can no longer speak to their grandchildren, and the descriptive nuances and sense of humour change. What we end up with is a pan-Indian culture that has the English language at its base.

How did we end up in this sorry situation? There are two answers. The first is easy. The residential school experience led us to believe that our languages were substandard and archaic. Children who attended residential schools learned the language at home but weren't allowed to speak it at school. The result was a stunted development of the Native languages, where they spoke like little children even though they were young adults. After a few years back on the reserve, however, their language skills grew.

With the migration to urban centres, the language of the home has become English. In the cities, families are often on their own. Grandparents are back on the reserve, and the family unit that would normally speak their language has been broken up.

Second and harder to accept is that we did it to ourselves. Like any parent, Aboriginal parents want what is best for their kids, and they felt that learning their language would hold the children back in school. The fact is that a second language is a great learning tool.

Many Aboriginal parents are no different from immigrant parents. They feel that their language will not help their children succeed at school and in life. The reality is that bilingual people have another perspective and generally do better in school.

But the great killer of Aboriginal languages is television. It was welcomed into our homes. It was revered and given a place of honour, and we sat and watched it for hours.

The television has done more damage to our languages than any government policy or other piece of technology. It permeates the home. English becomes the language of daily usage, and in the end we pay with our language and culture.

The invention of satellite technology is another nail in the coffin. Now people living in remote communities can have access to the hundred-channel universe and bring the English-speaking world into their home. Not only is the language foreign, but the content is worlds away. How do Aboriginal people in Fond du Lac react to a story about a bunch of self-absorbed New Yorkers or middle-class young people in some American city?

It is a recipe for a single monoculture. This is globalization, and in the end we are all expected to be consumers in a white middle-class American world. English is the language of commerce and culture, and other languages are redundant. Smaller cultures just get in the way and end up like bugs on the windshield of the relentless drive to globalization.

Today Aboriginal languages are taught in schools, but the real battleground is the home. Aboriginal parents must speak their language to their children and turn off the TV; otherwise, the next generation will lose out on our rich heritage.

Television has helped in the Americanization of Canada because of the proliferation of American programming and the saturation of American culture. But it was also there for the first moon landing, Diana's funeral, and the tragedy of 9/11. Television is a window on the world, but whose world, and in whose language?

Television is more than a benign wasteland. It attacks our languages and introduces foreign cultural values into First Nations society. In many homes, in all cultures, the television has become the one-eyed baby-sitter. Children are placed in front of it in the hope that they will stay out of trouble.

For Aboriginal people, it has served as a powerful communications tool and a doorway to another culture. But television has made English the operating language in the home. Parents don't communicate with their children in their first language any more. English has taken over, and television was the Trojan horse that let it happen. We welcomed television into our homes; we went into debt to get one, and, if we didn't have one, we went and visited the neighbours. And in the end, it ate away at our language and culture and gave us little in return.

When the Aboriginal Peoples Television Network (APTN) was inaugurated a few years ago, many believed that some help was in store for Aboriginal culture and languages. But the issue is too great for one national institution. There are fifty-two Aboriginal languages in Canada, and only four have a large enough population to assure their long-term survival. If we look at the concerted effort the government undertook to preserve and strengthen the French language, then a massive effort is needed to preserve Aboriginal languages.

Other national programs like the Telefilm Aboriginal Languages Program have helped. It has been accessed by Aboriginal producers and is an important resource in the battle to save our languages.

The battle for our fair share continues. We have very little programming on the mainstream channels. The amount of time devoted to Aboriginal issues is pitiful. When we make the news it is more often because of a car accident, corruption, or some spectacular crime. Very seldom are we shown in a positive light. This rubs off on the public, and a negative perception has developed whenever Aboriginal issues come up. We are seen as a problem rather than part of the solution.

APTN is our national broadcaster, and under the terms of their CRTC licence they receive a portion of the cable subscription to fund their operations. APTN reaches into over eight million homes and provides a window on the Aboriginal world. This new broadcaster has experienced some growing pains like any other new broadcaster, but in the end I see it performing a valuable service for greater understanding and improved race relations.

Profile – Anahareo

Saskatchewan history is full of colourful characters, and one of the most celebrated is the naturalist Grey Owl. But few people are aware of the woman behind the myth of Grey Owl.

Anahareo was Grey Owl's partner for ten stormy years and lived with him in northern Ontario, Riding Mountain National Park in Manitoba, and Prince Albert National Park in Saskatchewan.

Anahareo was also known as Gertrude Bernard, a Mohawk whose family originally came from Oka, Quebec. Anahareo was her Mohawk name; it means wild grapes.

She was raised outside the reserve in the Ottawa Valley town of Mattawa. Her mother died when she was only four, and she was raised by her grandparents. When they were too old to care for her, she moved in with her aunt and uncle.

Anahareo planned to go to college in Toronto, but in 1925 she was working as a waitress in a tourist camp on Lake Temagami when she meet a white man masquerading as an Indian called Grey Owl. His real name was Archie Belaney, and he came from Hastings, England.

The fact that Grey Owl was not an Indian was never a secret as far as Indian people were concerned. He spoke Cree and Ojibwa with an accent and didn't look like an Indian. But if that's what he wanted to do, nobody seemed to complain.

Anyway, Archie and Gertrude became an item and set up housekeeping. Archie was a woodsman, a hunter, a trapper, and a guide. Archie had been married before in England and had lived with an Indian woman in northern Ontario, and they had a son. But Anahareo was to become the great love of his life. Still, they had a rocky relationship and separated on more than one occasion.

In reality, Grey Owl was a very flawed individual. He drank too much and was abusive toward Anahareo. He was very insecure and had not had a successful permanent relationship. Like Anahareo, he had not been raised by his parents; in his case, his two aunts in Hastings had looked after him.

During the winter they went out on the trapline and Anahareo became disgusted with the cruelty of trapping animals for their pelts. She had been raised in town, so this kind of life was foreign to her.

Once Grey Owl killed a beaver, and two kits were orphaned as a result. Anahareo kept them and named them Jelly Roll and Rawhide. They lived in the lake beside their cabin. It was really Anahareo who convinced Grey Owl to become a naturalist and conservationist. She was his inspiration and his passion.

Grey Owl's moods and drinking often got the better of her and she would leave and go prospecting in northern Quebec. Later, when they lived in Waskesiu, she would head north and work as a prospector on the Churchill River.

In 1931, Archie Belaney started to work for the Parks Branch, first at

Riding Mountain in Manitoba and later at Prince Albert National Park.

Grey Owl and Anahareo found both happiness and fame at Ajawaan Lake in Saskatchewan. By now, Grey Owl was busy writing his books and Anahareo had given birth to their daughter, Dawn.

In spite of this, Grey Owl would head into Prince Albert and go on a binge. His health was not good, his heart was weak, but he became a common sight on a drunk in PA. Here was a white man reinforcing the stereotype of a drunken Indian.

After a while, Anahareo sent Dawn to live with friends in Prince Albert so Dawn could get an education. Anahareo left Archie and went north prospecting. Grey Owl's fame continued to increase.

In 1936 and '37, he returned to England on a speaking tour, where he played the role of a famous Indian naturalist. He continued to drink, and his handlers were always trying to keep him under control.

All the time he was suffering from tuberculosis, and in 1938 he died.

Anahareo became a forgotten person. The racism and sexism of the times would not allow people to recognize her as the driving force behind the development of Grey Owl the naturalist. She was just one more Indian woman who would not receive fair treatment.

She was the little Mohawk girl who left her homeland and travelled far to the west at a time when Indian people seldom left their reserve. She was a very special person.

Profile – Bernelda Wheeler

Pioneers pay a high price for their commitment. They are the ones who have to go out and break the trail, set up the camp, and face all the negative elements.

Bernelda Wheeler was one of our pioneers in the field of Aboriginal journalism. She died on September 10, 2005, in Saskatoon after a long battle with cancer. I worked with her and visited her over the years, and I could see that her cancer was taking its toll in spite of hopes that it was going into remission.

She was born on the Muscowpetung First Nation in 1937. Her parents were from the George Gordon First Nation but they travelled widely, living in Herb Lake and Churchill, Manitoba.

Her career in radio began early, and at seventeen she was a disc jockey for CHFC in Churchill, which was an affiliate with the CBC Northern Service. She worked briefly as a practical nurse, and in the late 1960s she returned to CBC, this time as the host, producer, and investigative journalist for "Our Native Land" with CBC national radio.

Her years with this program defined her as one of Canada's leading Aboriginal journalists. I recall listening to "Our Native Land" while I was away from home at university. It was the only program in the country that dealt with news of our people. I remember that Bernelda's was the only Aboriginal voice that I heard hosting any radio or television program.

In 1982 she received a special award as the First Lady of Native Broadcasting in Canada and was twice nominated for ACTRA awards for best writer and best radio program.

In 1992 she appeared on CBC Newsworld as the moderator for the candidates' debate for the national chief of the Assembly of First Nations. Her professional approach and sense of fairness came through, and the debate was seen by many as the first chance for a national audience to become aware of First Nations issues.

Bernelda continued to participate in the media. She wrote numerous newspaper articles and wrote a column for Saskatchewan's *Eaglefeather News*. She also wrote short stories, poetry, and children's books, receiving the Children's Choice and Toronto Children's Book awards.

Bernelda was a true storyteller in the First Nations tradition. She also discovered a passion for acting as another way of telling our stories, appearing in the iconic play "The Rez Sisters." She also played the role of one of Big Bear's wives in the CBC miniseries "Big Bear."

But Bernelda was not one who was content to only tell stories. She also wanted to be a part of them and a part of the movement for change that is sweeping Indian Country. Back when she lived in Winnipeg she was one of the founding members of the National Association of Friendship Centres. She was also an active member of Grandmothers for Justice. Later she would be recognized for her community work, receiving the 2002 Citizen of the Year award in the FSIN Circle of Honour and the 2005 Elizabeth Fry Society's "Rebel with a Cause" award.

The year she died, the Anskohk Aboriginal Literature Festival presented her family with a posthumous lifetime achievement award.

Bernelda's strength and tenacity rubbed off on her two children, Jordan and Winona. As a single mother, Bernelda raised the two in Winnipeg and saw them embark on successful careers. Jordan Wheeler is an accomplished screenwriter with credits that include story editor for "North of Sixty" and scripts for "The Rez," "Black Harbour," and "Renegade Press." Winona Wheeler is an academic who did her undergraduate work at the University of Manitoba and went on to receive her doctorate in history at the University of Southern California, Berkley. She was dean of the Saskatoon campus of the First Nations University of Canada until she was unceremoniously fired as a part of the FSIN purge in 2005.

Bernelda was a role model to many, and her good works can be seen in the number of Aboriginal journalists that are succeeding in media across the country. It can be seen in the number of women attending university and people who stand up to injustice. Pioneers like Bernelda pay a price, but on the other hand they make the world a better place.

CHAPTER FOUR

RIGHTS AND SELF-GOVERNMENT

First Nations self-government isn't about running casinos or selling cheap cigarettes. It's about the future of our people and meeting their needs. It's a future that all Saskatchewan residents will share. First Nations self-government must once again be brought to the attention of the public. Since 1982, our population has doubled in Saskatchewan, and we now command much more political power than at any time in our recent history.

The Constitution and Jurisdiction, Yet to Be Determined

In 1982, First Nations, Métis, and Inuit leaders successfully negotiated recognition of treaty and Aboriginal rights in Canada's Charter of Rights and Freedoms. It was considered both a turning point in history and an empty promise.

Since then, we have seen both scenarios. The Charter was the first time we received legal recognition of our Aboriginal and treaty rights in the constitution, but these rights were undefined. That has been the focus of court cases over the past two decades.

Section 35 in the Canadian Charter of Rights and Freedoms states that "existing Treaty and Aboriginal rights are hereby recognized and affirmed." There are two groups of rights that are included in this section.

First, Treaty rights go back over a century when Canada was expanding westward. In Saskatchewan and Alberta, a series of treaties, known as the numbered treaties, were negotiated. These treaties guaranteed education, health care, social services, and economic assistance, among other rights.

Second, Aboriginal or inherent rights include those rights that we kept or were not on the table for negotiation when the treaties were signed. These include rights such as keeping our language, culture, and religion. We maintained jurisdiction over our land and our people. The very act of signing a treaty indicates recognition of our leadership and right to make decisions on our own behalf.

The original constitutional negotiations allowed for a series of First Ministers' conferences that were supposed to define what was meant by treaty and Aboriginal rights. These conferences turned out to be an abject failure because there was no political will on the part of the premiers. Saskatchewan's Premier Grant Devine was especially intransigent. He claimed that the province was spending a million dollars a day on Indians but he wasn't prepared to help define self-government.

The 1987 First Ministers' conference was such a shambles of bad faith and apathy that it prompted Métis leader Jim Sinclair to blast the premiers in his now famous closing remarks. It wasn't pretty but it was widely supported by Aboriginal people across the country because it reflected the widespread frustration that was and still is out there. He criticized BC Premier Bill Vander Zalm for his remarks that his family came from Holland following the Second World War. Jim reminded him that our people fought and died in record numbers to help liberate his country and they deserved better from him. But he saved his most cutting remarks for Grant Devine, accusing him of receiving one billion dollars from the federal government to "buy an election." For many, it was our generation's equivalent of Dr. Martin Luther King's "I Have a Dream" speech.

With the absence of serious commitment from the provinces, the definition of our rights and self-government came from two other sources. The courts gave it a broad definition, but the federal government, through the Department of Indian Affairs, treated self-government as self-administration. Indian Affairs's version of self-government is to take the obsolete and outdated practices of the department and transfer them to the First Nations. It's neocolonialism for the twenty-first century.

This is where we stand today. The courts have recognized the rights of off-reserve Indians in the *Corbiere* case, recognized First Nations land rights in *Delgamuukw,* and when the White Bear First Nation in Saskatchewan went to court over its right to establish a casino, the court found in its favour. The threat of court action led to the Treaty Land Entitlement Agreement between twenty-five Saskatchewan First Nations, the Saskatchewan government, and the federal government in 1992.

The real conflict in self-government is between the provinces and the First Nations. That's why jurisdictional issues have the provinces tied up in knots. If the First Nations take the provincial governments to court, the provinces will lose because they have no jurisdiction in Indian Country. Under the BNA Act, the federal government has responsibility for "Indians, and Lands reserved for the Indians." The jurisdictions of the provinces and the First Nations overlap in many areas, and the provinces have yet to come to grips with this reality.

Of course, recognition and implementation are two different issues. While the Charter of Rights and Freedoms granted recognition of our rights, it has taken the courts to force the issue. This has been an expensive and time-consuming process, and our people continue to languish in poverty with health and social issues.

Self-government Comes from Within

American President George Bush has this naive idea that he can send his troops to other countries and "spread freedom."

Bush's plan to spread democracy or else is a cause for some concern. Everyone wants democracy. It's like motherhood. If you stand against the spread of democracy, you look like some sort of anarchist or communist or worse.

But it's a fundamental fact that lasting social change begins from the bottom and moves up. If change is imposed, it is shallow, lacks nutrition, and doesn't take root. The Americans' misadventure in Iraq is an example of forced change going horribly wrong.

My experience with change is first-hand and dates back to the early 1970s when the Federation of Saskatchewan Indians took over a community development program that had been run by the Department of Indian Affairs. It consisted of assistance for local government and other help to band councils.

Under the direction of the Federation of Saskatchewan Indians, it became an agent for change. Community development workers assisted band councils as they had in the past, but this time they were directly responsible to the local people and they carried out their agenda for change. Community development became an activist program, and it laid the groundwork for self-government with Saskatchewan First Nations.

In the past, the opposite had been the case: there was no shortage of outside influences. The government, through the Department of Indian Affairs, carried out policies that told our people what they could do, which in the early years included such trivia as who could sell farm produce, who could leave the reserve, and if religious ceremonies could be held.

Reserves were usually either Catholic or Anglican. In some cases, missionaries fought over souls on the same reserve, causing division and hard feelings that exist to the present day.

But the children were the ones who suffered most. Residential schools swallowed up whole communities of children in a vain attempt to civilize and Christianize the next generation. Later, the children would be caught in the "big scoop," with welfare agencies removing children from their families and placing them in non-Indian homes across the country and in the United States and Europe.

Today's social problems among our people are largely a result of our losing control of our lives. Other people doing what they thought was best for us has done us a lot of damage.

The best example of meaningful long-term change coming from the people is the movement to establish Indian control of education in the 1970s. People on reserves withdrew their children from the local integrated schools and established their own on-reserve education centres. Today there are numerous schools on reserves, and the education rate of our people has risen considerably.

The education movement of the 1970s was the spark that lit the flame of self-government. It came from the people and it had deep roots.

If you look back at the past fifty years of First Nations history, you will see a trail of change that was forced by our people themselves. We lobbied to have our rights recognized in the Charter of Rights and Freedoms, and we continue to fight for self-government, treaty rights, and political rights.

Today, First Nations are developing their own constitutions and creating self-government based on their own cultural and social norms. This is not being imposed; it comes from the people. The only way self-government will be successful is if it continues to come from the people.

Every so often the Canadian government comes forward with so-called self-government legislation, but it comes with strings attached. It is really self-administration, or worse, neo-colonialism, with the chiefs and councils acting as the new Indian agents.

Meaningful change must come from the people at the local level. Change imposed is change bound to fail. Today, First Nations have their own education system, we have our own land tenure, we have our own election procedures, and our religion is coming back. This is change that flies in the face of a century of forced government and religious interference.

So when I hear people like George Bush saying that he will bring democracy to the rest of the world, I see more people losing control over their lives. I see the American army trying to force fundamental social change at the point of a gun, and I know it simply won't work. Spreading freedom is the new colonialism.

People resent others telling them what to do, and that is a lesson that George Bush – and the Canadian government – will learn the hard way.

A Charter Challenge Affects Us All

The debate over same-sex marriage is a cause for some concern for Aboriginal people, not over the issue itself but over the method proposed to override the legislation. Alberta Premier Ralph Klein has stated that he will invoke the notwithstanding clause in the constitution to prevent the legislation from becoming a reality in his province.

As a Treaty First Nations person, I shudder when I hear politicians announce the cavalier use of the notwithstanding clause. It cheapens the spirit of the Charter of Rights and Freedoms and is a steep and slippery slope for Aboriginal peoples whose rights are protected there.

In 2005, the Liberal government tabled legislation in the House of Commons that extended the right to marry to same-sex couples. In response, Stephen Harper, who was the opposition leader at the time, stated that he would oppose the legislation and propose amendments to allow for a marriage act that excluded same-sex couples. In an open letter to Harper, 133 law professors pointed out that Harper's strategy was flawed and would simply place the issue back in the courts.

The courts in British Columbia, Saskatchewan, Manitoba, Newfoundland, Ontario, Quebec, Nova Scotia, and the Yukon have all ruled that a definition of marriage that excludes same-sex couples is unconstitutional. The Charter of Rights and

Freedoms clearly states that everyone in Canada has fundamental freedoms. Section 15 of the Charter states that "every individual is equal before and under the law... without discrimination based on race, national or ethnic origin, colour, religion, sex, age or mental or physical disability."

The right wing has used the term "activist judges" when referring to court decisions they don't agree with. The reality is that the courts are making decisions based on the Charter of Rights and Freedoms which is part of the Canadian constitution and is the bedrock of the law in this country. When political parties discount the legal system and the laws of the land because they don't suit their narrow agenda, how strong are our legal institutions?

Aboriginal people have their rights protected in section 35 of the Charter. When politicians make loose talk about avoiding or ignoring the constitution, we need to take a serious look at their respect for the constitution and other rights and freedoms. In 1982 when the Charter was passed, our analysis was that it gave us the right to go to court. In hindsight, we were right, and in the intervening years the courts have made numerous decisions in support of our rights, but supporting legislation has failed to keep pace. In British Columbia, the historic *Delgamuukw* decision recognized First Nations title to the land, but movement toward a treaty settlement is still stalled.

For the past twenty-five years we have been caught between the courts and the politicians as we attempt to gain jurisdiction, self-government and recognition for our treaty rights. Now, if the Conservatives have their way, the issue of gay marriage will be caught in that dead zone between positive legal opinions and reluctant politicians.

But if you stand back and take a dispassionate look at gay marriage, why is it such a big deal? It won't affect me in the least. I'm in a traditional marriage. If it poses some kind of threat then maybe marriage isn't as secure an institution as we might hope. I think it's very selfish and narrow-minded of some people to deny happiness and security to other people based only on their sexual preference. And let's remember that the government legislation is only for civil marriages. If individual churches refuse to recognize same-sex unions then that is their business.

If you believe the rhetoric of the Conservative Party, you get the idea that same-sex marriage is the biggest threat to Canadians. This leaves the impression that we must live in a pretty great country if this is the biggest issue facing politicians. Harper has fought an increasingly confusing campaign against same-sex marriage. First he stated that it would open the door for polygamy, and recently when speaking to an assembly of Sikhs he stated that it would mean the end of Canadian multiculturalism. Harper is going to the wall on this issue as if it were the most important issue facing Canadians. And now that he is prime minister, he is determined to hold a free vote on the issue in parliament.

What about child poverty, drug addiction, care for the elderly, and homeless kids on the street? These issues have fallen off the national agenda while the focus remains on same-sex marriage.

But at the end of the day, the sun will rise in the east and set in the west. People will continue to fall in love and get married, and some will be of the same sex.

Asserting Sovereignty, but at What Cost?

In the early 1970s I worked for the Alberta Native Communications Society in Edmonton. This Christmas I received a letter from an old friend who brought me up to date about what had happened to the old crowd. Two of my old colleagues are dead from lung cancer and two more have it. Cancer is a modern-day plague, and our people are suffering.

Back then it seemed like everyone smoked and there were few restrictions. You couldn't smoke near an oxygen tent or when fueling an airplane, but that was pretty much it. The short-term fear of an explosion was considered more important than the long-term health costs. Today we are aware of the link between smoking and cancer and the tragic human cost associated with smoking.

I was therefore not very happy to hear that the chiefs of the Federation of Saskatchewan Indian Nations (FSIN) will not be enforcing a smoking ban in their casinos.

This is an issue with two sides. On one hand it is a health issue, and on the other it is an issue of First Nations jurisdiction. The chiefs and the FSIN have stated that they have to assert their sovereignty and jurisdiction and that provincial laws don't apply on reserves. I support this idea in principle, but there's such a thing as a fight not worth having. Is this one?

The battle for jurisdiction has been on-going for years – the initial flap over gaming was based on jurisdiction. The province insisted that gaming was their jurisdiction and the First Nations insisted it was otherwise. The result was a negotiated settlement that allowed for First Nations casinos.

In other cases, provincial laws are applied by default. In the absence of First Nations legislation, the province steps in. Child adoption and welfare regulations are examples of provincial jurisdiction that have been forced on First Nations. Also, schools have to use the provincial curriculum if their students are to be accepted in post-secondary institutions.

Over the years there has been a steady encroachment of provincial jurisdiction on First Nations. The process needs to be reversed, but an exception to the province-wide smoking ban is not the answer, for two reasons.

First, it is a good law. The chiefs should assert their jurisdiction by adopting the outright ban on smoking in public places. It's not as if it would be anything new. Many band offices are smoke-free, and the office buildings on the Muskeg Lake urban reserve in Saskatoon are all smoke-free by order of the Muskeg Lake Band Council.

Second, the public is not on our side this time. Smokers are the lepers of the twenty-first century, and everything possible is being done to ban smoking. The majority of the public wants to see smoking banned in public places. As First Nations we need all the support we can get, and throwing away goodwill is not in our best interest.

Adopting a new position will not be as easy as simply making a decree that First Nations buildings will be smoke-free. The FSIN has a policy of respecting the sovereignty of individual First Nations. Each First Nation is sovereign, and no amount of posturing on the part of the provincial leadership will change that. The First Nation that owns the land the casino occupies must therefore adopt a band by-law making their institutions and businesses smoke-free. Simply complying with provincial legislation is not an option. It's a false hope that FSIN Chief Alphonse Bird can simply wave a magic wand and the situation will be solved.

The provincial government has mishandled this situation badly. The First Nations were not involved in any consultations and discussions, and the province simply assumed that the First Nations would comply. The province seriously underestimated the process that First Nations have to follow to create laws and exercise self-government. If the First Nations had been involved from the beginning, this whole issue could have been worked out in advance.

The New Democratic Party has taken First Nations for granted by spreading fear of the Saskatchewan Party. If you criticize NDP policies or actions, the NDP are quick to point out, "What about those guys? They'd do a whole lot worse!" As a result, First Nations voters have gone to the polls and supported the lesser evil.

The province's minister of First Nations and Métis Relations, Maynard Sonntag, has only made the situation worse with his ham-fisted remark that the minister of Indian Affairs should get involved and disallow band by-laws. This can only be perceived as more of the old colonialism, with the Department of Indian Affairs being asked to take on the role of the old-time Indian agent.

Both sides are drawing lines in the sand, and in the process a good law is being used as a pawn by both sides to assert their power.

The two sides need to sit down and work out an agreement that is in the best interests of all Saskatchewan residents. Cancer is an equal-opportunity killer that doesn't recognize racial differences. We need to recognize that and pick a fight worth having.

Self-government Must Evolve in Order to Grow

The Federation of Saskatchewan Indian Nations (FSIN) has reached an important step in the evolution of First Nations self-government. The role of the chiefs has to be upgraded from administrators to policy-makers. It's time that our leaders returned to their traditional roles.

The traditional role of the chiefs was to be a moral and spiritual leader for their band of followers. More specialized duties such as warrior leader or shaman were taken by other leaders who held special powers. Leaders were selected by the people for their special talents.

Following the signing of the treaties and North-West Resistance, many First Nations didn't have chiefs. Indian Affairs controlled every aspect of First Nations decision-making and often refused to recognize legitimate leaders. For example, Indian Affairs refused to allow the Beardy's band to elect a chief because of their alleged role in the battle of Duck Lake. For over thirty years, the band was without a chief.

From the 1930s to the 1950s when political leaders began organizing the League of Saskatchewan Indians and later the Union of Saskatchewan Indians, many bands didn't have chiefs. It was the duty of the early leaders to assist First Nations to select their leadership. Many chiefs were traditional lifetime chiefs and later they had to comply with the election provisions in the Indian Act.

It was a political decision on the part of the early leaders to build up the office of the chiefs. Indian Affairs found it harder and harder to exercise their dictatorial power as the First Nations became more and more democratic and placed their collective power in the hands of a chief and councillors.

Over the years, the Department of Indian Affairs has devolved their programs to the First Nations and, in the process, attempted to bureaucratize the role of the chief and council. Today, band councils administer millions of dollars and do the job of the Department of Indian Affairs. They have the responsibility but no authority. That is still held by the Department of Indian Affairs.

First Nations now contain thousands of people and their administrations handle millions of dollars annually. This is a far cry from the original chiefs that signed the treaties.

In addition to their duties at the local level, the chiefs control their provincial organization, the Federation of Saskatchewan Indian Nations, which includes a wide variety of institutions that deliver economic, educational, and social services. All these institutions have boards of directors made up of chiefs.

The First Nations University of Canada has a thirty-one member board of governors and about three-quarters are chiefs. Meanwhile, the University of Saskatchewan has a twelve member board of governors. The original plan back in the early 1980s was that the chiefs would have a temporary role as board members to establish the long-term policies and direction of the institution. Once it was established, the chiefs would step back and the boards would be staffed with First Nations educators and specialists. Instead, the chiefs' influence on the board of governors has grown and become entrenched.

There needs to be an evaluation of the role of chiefs on boards. There is too much micromanaging and not enough time spent addressing the big picture. The First Nations University has to grow and develop with the times. Right now, it is poised to become a major international educational leader. It can become the Oxford of the First Nations, but it must be given room to grow. There is a crying need to allow for academic freedom for both the staff and students. Students should be encouraged to speak out and question authority. Questioning and criticizing politicians, administrators, and elders are an important part of a person's education.

The chiefs must now move away from micromanaging and work in policy and priority areas. Being administrators is a comfortable rut but it leads nowhere.

Today, our leaders have issues and challenges that are far greater than a few decades ago when the institutions were established. Our leaders need to address major policy issues like justice, policing, urban chaos, and protection of treaty rights. Two decades ago, alcohol was a major addictions problem; today, addictions include crack, heroin, and crystal meth, and it's killing our people. The urban areas are a new front for political action. Welfare, unemployment, drug addiction, and gang activity are creating special problems in the urban areas.

On the other end of the spectrum, First Nations companies and economic institutions are rapidly increasing in importance. We need to increase our economic activity to accommodate our rapidly increasing labour force.

There are also a series of positive court cases that require follow-up if we are to occupy important areas of jurisdiction.

The chiefs and the FSIN must rethink their role. We cannot allow our leaders to spin their wheels as administrators when there is so much important work to be done. The chiefs should look at forming policy committees to develop legislation and policy much like parliamentary committees. We need less micromanaging and a more professional approach to serious issues that face our people.

Painful Parallels

"Back in 2002 I wrote a newspaper column expressing my support for the Palestinian people. I took what I thought was a dispassionate view of the situation, but my editors thought differently. The column was "spiked" – pulled by the editors – and was picked up by Prairie Dog *magazine. I became a cause célèbre. I did the column in all honesty and naiveté, thinking that my point of view had merit and would trigger discussion, because isn't generating heat the role of a columnist? I was both right and*

wrong. It triggered discussion, but around the issue of owner inter-
ference in the editorial content of newspapers. Somehow the issue
I was trying to raise, the plight of the Palestinians and the com-
parison to my people's situation, was lost in the controversy."

Often I find myself watching the events on the world stage
from a First Nations' perspective. The ongoing conflict
between the Palestinians and the Israelis is a case in point. What
we have here is a complicated land claim without any claims
commission to work things out.

The problem revolves around the fact that the state of Israel
was created on land formerly known as Palestine. The former
inhabitants were removed from the land. After two thousand
years of inhabiting the area, you'd think that the Palestinians had
a pretty good claim on the land. I know it would hold up if it
were reviewed by the Canadian Indian Claims Commission.

Over the years, I have maintained a sympathetic point of
view toward the Palestinians. I see them as the Indians of the
Middle East.

Their history is hauntingly familiar. The Palestinians lost their
land, they were placed in refuge camps similar to reservations,
and they were colonized and controlled by an outside force. As
a First Nations person in Canada, I see an enormous parallel.

In Canada we have decades of treaty entitlements and land
claims, and if we have learned anything it's that these issues don't
go away. If one generation can't negotiate a settlement, then the
next one will be better educated and take the issue to court. If
that generation is unable to get a settlement, then we are looking at blockades and more militant action. The claim will grow
in size and cost with each generation. It won't go away. If anything, it gains moral and political strength and hardens the
resolve of our people.

This is the same case for the Palestinian people. The dream of their own state has remained unchanged for the past fifty years, and no amount of oppression will take it away. With any colonized people, the flame of independence only burns brighter with the passage of time.

In our case, the difference is that Canada has recognized Aboriginal and treaty rights in the constitution and Charter of Rights and Freedoms. Mechanisms like the Indian Claims Commission have been developed to find solutions. In Saskatchewan, we have the Office of the Treaty Commissioner, which successfully negotiated the Treaty Land Entitlement Agreement.

The Israelis also built their nation on other people's land, but they regard any sign of dissent as terrorism. This is common practice. The demonization of a people is a blunt instrument used to get the public on side. As a First Nations person, I have witnessed attacks on our leadership by groups such as the Taxpayers Federation and the Conservative party. These attacks are personal and inflammatory and produce a visceral response from those unable to make up their own mind.

Over the years, the United States has supported the State of Israel, alienating itself from the larger Middle Eastern community. American and Canadian media carry a definite bias toward Israel, and at times they can be racist in their condemnation of the Palestinians.

In Canada, we are not well informed. The media picks up news from the extremes such as the Jewish settlers and terrorist organizations on both sides. It's a little like learning about Christianity by getting information from the Knights of the Ku Klux Klan or fundamentalist demagogues like Jerry Falwell or Pat Robertson.

In this climate there is no negotiating to recognize land claims or self-government. The settlers continue to move into

the West Bank, land that doesn't technically belong to them. Overcrowding continues in the Palestinian camps, and people live in poverty with little hope for the future. Even the use of the word "settlers" indicates a Wild West mentality and strengthens the parallel between our two groups.

Because the issue remains unresolved and continues to fester, the cause has been picked up by radical groups. It's no fluke that Hamas was elected to lead the country in 2006. The cause of Palestinian nationalism has been picked up by Muslim fundamentalists, and the Palestinian Christian minority has been pushed aside.

Unresolved issues become radicalized as options run out. Here in Canada we see that the First Nations leadership in British Columbia are more outspoken because of their frustration with the government's intransigence in the treaty negotiation process and their lack of a settlement.

I'll probably be accused of being anti-Semitic, but that is not the case. I am against any group of people pushing another nation off their traditional land. It's a story my people have lived for seven generations. It's a problem that has no easy solution, but both sides must work together in an atmosphere of respect or this story will never end.

Profile – Harold Cardinal

They say that intellectuals are an important part of any revolution, and the past several decades have seen a revolution in Indian Country. One of our prominent First Nations leaders and intellectuals was Dr. Harold Cardinal, who died of cancer in Edmonton on June 3, 2005.

My first journalism position was with the Alberta Native Communications Society in 1969. It was an exciting time because the

Indian political movement was in its infancy and it seemed like we were in the middle of a renaissance. The leading light in the renaissance was Harold Cardinal, the young president of the Indian Association of Alberta.

Harold came from the Sucker Creek reserve in northern Alberta. He had attended St. Francis Xavier University in Nova Scotia and was considered by many to be the leader that could jump-start the Indian movement in Alberta as well as across the country.

Pierre Elliott Trudeau had been elected leader of the Liberal Party and Trudeaumania was a political fact. This was the golden age for the Liberals. They were even getting elected in Alberta. When Harold was elected leader of Alberta's Indians at age twenty-three, the press picked up on it as another Trudeau phenomenon. Harold was the darling of the media.

One night, Harold Cardinal, a reporter, and Minister of Health John Munro were travelling on a country road. They were pulled over by the RCMP and questions were asked. Who were they? What were they doing? It was routine for Harold but an eye-opener for the health minister and the reporter. I spoke to John Munro years later and he told me that that incident was something he would never forget.

But the stage became crowded in 1969 when a naive young Indian Affairs minister, Jean Chrétien, allowed his bureaucrats to write Indian policy. The 1969 white paper was the sorry result. The white paper called for the end to federal responsibility and the dumping of Indians and our lands on the provinces.

Harold Cardinal and the Indian association swung into action and, after a period of consultation, they developed the "Red Paper" to counter the "White Paper." The Alberta chiefs went to Ottawa and presented the paper to the prime minister, who told them the white paper would be shelved and a more moderate process would be undertaken. He stated that they could wait as long as twenty years for a new plan.

Twenty-two years later we would see treaty and Aboriginal rights entrenched in the Charter of Rights and Freedoms.

In addition to his political work, Cardinal was a published author. His book *The Unjust Society* took direct aim at the failed policies of the federal government and was a poke at Trudeau's remark to make Canada a "just society." His book became the reference book of the next generation of First Nations leaders. Even today it is required reading for Native studies classes.

Following his time in politics, Harold Cardinal became a leading intellectual. He was retained by First Nations political organizations and taught at the University of Saskatchewan. He completed his L.L.M. – Masters of Law – degree at Harvard and in 1999 received an honorary Doctorate in Law at the University of Alberta. He was working on his doctorate at the University of British Columbia at the time of his death.

Harold's landmark work *Treaty Elders of Saskatchewan* outlines the First Nations concept of the treaties as seen through the eyes and memory of the elders. The book was so comprehensive that it was used as a guide by the FSIN for the treaty implementation in Saskatchewan.

Among his many accomplishments, he was awarded a lifetime achievement award by the National Aboriginal Achievement Foundation.

Harold created definitions and expressions that still stand today. He saw Aboriginal people as "the red tile in the Canadian mosaic," equal but distinct. He called First Nations people "citizens plus" in reference to our treaty rights. And ignorance and bigotry formed the "buckskin curtain" that held our people back.

Harold Cardinal was a leader who was at the right place at the right time. He was a leader who was able to combat the federal government at crucial time in our history, and he went on to become one of the truly great First Nations leaders and intellectuals of the twentieth century.

Profile – Gladys Johnston

Gladys Johnston was buried on the Mistawasis First Nation in close proximity to her parents, Joe and Evelyn Dreaver, and her great-great-grandfather, Chief Mistawasis. She was a member of a famous First

Nations family, and her life closely paralleled First Nations history for most of the twentieth century.

She was born on April 7, 1920, the daughter of Chief Joe Dreaver of the Mistawasis First Nation. Later she attended the File Hills residential school on the Okanese First Nation and the Brandon residential school in Manitoba. She joined the Royal Canadian Air Force during the Second World War.

She was following in her father's footsteps. The Dreaver family paid a heavy price for their contribution to Canada. Joe Dreaver was in the army during World War One and received the military medal for bravery at Ypres. He lost a brother at the battle of Vimy Ridge and another brother was sent home from wounds he received at the same battle.

When war broke out in Europe he encouraged the young men on the reserve to sign up. One of the young men to sign up was his son Harvey. Joe also enlisted, and while he was past the age of overseas service, he served with the veterans guard at the prisoners of war facility in Medicine Hat, Alberta.

Harvey Dreaver was killed in action at the battle of the Leopold Canal in Belgium and was buried in the Adegem war cemetery. Harvey was a sergeant, and following his death the Belgian government awarded him the Belgian Croix de Guerre for "outstanding contributions toward the liberation of Belgium." The loss of her big brother weighed heavy on Gladys, and she never really got over it.

Following the war, Gladys returned to a life where the freedom that they had fought for didn't exist for her own people. This was the challenge of the returning veterans. They knew what freedom was, and the days of the old Indian agents were limited. In 1946 Gladys attended the founding meeting of the Union of Saskatchewan Indians and was elected the organization's secretary-treasurer. This organization was led by the late John Tootoosis and was the forerunner of the Federation of Saskatchewan Indian Nations. There had been other attempts to organize on a regional level but the union was the first organization that included all the First Nations in the province.

Her interest in politics extended beyond First Nations politics, and for a while she worked as a secretary for John Diefenbaker. Like many educated people of her generation, she worked within the Department of Indian Affairs. At the time, there were no outside resources for Aboriginal people, so government provided an outlet for people who wanted to work on behalf of their communities.

Using her base in Indian Affairs, she assisted in the formation of the Saskatchewan Indian Women's Association. At the time, she was a community development officer and was able to provide resources to improve living conditions on reserves.

In 1961 she was among friends in a Battleford restaurant when she was told by the manager that they didn't serve Indians. She took the manager to court and won the case. It was the first time that a case of discrimination was won on our behalf. The owner had to pay a fine of twenty-five dollars.

Following the case, she got together with the RCMP and various members of the community who decided that something had to be done to improve race relations. She was appointed as the founding president of the Battlefords Indian Metis Friendship Centre. The centre is now an institution in the city of North Battleford, and its roots are in the good work of Gladys Johnston.

Her work as a political pioneer was recognized by the FSIN in 2004 at a chiefs' assembly in Yorkton. She received a star blanket for her role in the formation of the Union of Saskatchewan Indians.

Upon her retirement, she returned to her reserve and served two terms as a band councillor. She regarded the community as her home and the reserve residents as family. With her experience and insight she was able to provide valuable counsel to her chief, but her health deteriorated. She passed away in the Shellbrook hospital surrounded by her friends and family. She was eighty-five years old. Her death came only a week before her fifty-seventh wedding anniversary. She left behind her husband, Walter, and their eight children and numerous grandchildren.

Gladys Johnston was a true pioneer. She left a trail of good work, and we are better for it. We must never forget the contribution made by people of her generation who showed such strength and character in the face of overwhelming odds. The family is very aware of their special history, and in the words of her son Anthony, "the spirit is in each generation."

CHAPTER FIVE

STRUGGLES
AND SUCCESSES

Saskatchewan and indeed all of western Canada are undergoing rapid social change. For many it hasn't hit home yet, but for others it is no surprise. The rapidly increasing Aboriginal population demands human rights and socio-economic status equal to the non-Aboriginal population, and although it is still a struggle, because their political power increases with their size, they will succeed.

You're Number One, We're Not

When Jean Chrétien was prime minister, he loved to brag about Canada's ranking on the United Nations human development index. From 1966 to 2000 Canada was number one and over the years was continually in the top five of the best countries in the world in which to live.

The UN human development index combines the factors of education, literacy, life expectancy, and income to create an index that reflects the care and development of a nation's people. In 2004 the top country was Norway, followed by Sweden, Australia, and Canada. In 2005 Canada dropped to seventh place.

The United Nations released a report that takes First Nations people out of the equation. By themselves, Canada's First Nations are ranked at number forty-eight in the world. This puts us within the sphere of such countries as Croatia, Chile, Uruguay, and the United Arab Emirates.

The report, authored by Rodolfo Stavenhagen, the UN special rapporteur for Indigenous peoples, is the result of an official visit to Canada in 2004. Part of his research included conversations with federal and provincial authorities and representatives of Aboriginal peoples.

He found that Canada's Aboriginal people did not enjoy the good life of the rest of Canadians. In fact, he found that First Nations people here are consistently at the bottom of the social indicators.

For example, the annual income of Aboriginal people is "significantly lower" than other Canadians, and unemployment rates are much higher for Aboriginal people. Sixty percent of Aboriginal children live in poverty. In cities such as Winnipeg, 80 percent of inner-city Aboriginal households reported incomes under the poverty line.

On the health front, the gap in life expectancy between Aboriginal people and the rest of Canadians is 6.4 years. Aboriginal people suffer from higher rates of disease. The rate of tuberculosis is 6 times higher, heart disease is 1.5 times higher, and diabetes is 4 times higher. The leading cause of death for Aboriginal children and youth is suicide.

In the legal area, First Nations people represent 4.4 percent of the Canadian population but make up 17 percent of the prison population nationally. In other jurisdictions such as Saskatchewan and Manitoba, Aboriginal people make up 60 percent and more of the prison population.

First Nations women lack matrimonial and property rights, and suicide, prostitution, and child welfare issues have a particularly devastating effect on them.

On the other side, First Nations people in Canada enjoy constitutional recognition of their treaty and Aboriginal rights. This is unique in the world, but on the other hand, the government has been loath to implement those rights. The interpretation and enabling legislation has lagged far behind in spite of the fact that the courts have sided with the First Nations position on the treaties and the constitution.

The federal government only recognizes treaty rights on reserves in spite of the fact that now more than half of First Nations people live off the reserve. Civic and provincial governments are forced to pay for services to First Nations people although the constitution states that they are a federal responsibility.

Also, when First Nations enter into land claim negotiations they are required to "release" certain rights in order to reach a settlement. As a result, the claims process has been painfully slow, and few comprehensive claims have been concluded.

History has left Canada with a legacy of land claims, residential school claims, and a people badly damaged by colonialism.

It's shallow and premature to go around bragging about our good fortune when a significant part of the society is left out.

It's Crisis Time

The rapidly increasing Aboriginal population, particularly in this province's cities, can be seen as either a blessing or a serious problem depending on your point of view. Some see it as a source of a future labour force, while others see Aboriginal people as a problem who have no stake in the province's future.

The 2001 census from Statistics Canada points out the rapidly increasing urban Aboriginal population. Saskatoon leads the nation with a rate of growth of 382 percent, or a five-fold increase from 1981 to 2001. The rate of growth in Regina is 145 percent. The urban migration began in the 1960s in Regina, and the city experienced an earlier migration of Aboriginal people. In Saskatoon the migration was later, and the results indicate that.

The Aboriginal population has a much different demographic profile than the rest of the province. The median age for non-Aboriginal people in Saskatchewan is thirty-six; in other words, half the population is above and half below age thirty-six. For Aboriginal people, the median age is twenty years. While the non-Aboriginal population may be aging, the Aboriginal population is very young. Half our people were born after 1985.

This is placing stress on inner-city schools, which have a growing majority of Aboriginal children. As the population moves out to the suburbs, inner-city facilities usually fall into disuse. Instead, we see century-old buildings crammed with kids. The inner-city neighbourhoods are alive with a young Aboriginal population. Talk of falling enrolment for the First Nations University is actually the opposite. The enrolment is increasing simply through the pressure of a very young population. But that is a whole other topic.

The report from Statistics Canada also points out that Aboriginal youth between the ages of fifteen and twenty-four that wanted to enter the workforce had an employment rate of 35.2 percent and an unemployment rate of close to 25 percent. The remainder was either in school or not in the job market. These facts can only mean trouble. Frustration and poverty combine to increase the crime rate, and the solution is not to be found in increasing the size of the jails. Our young people need jobs if they are to progress and stay out of trouble.

Aboriginal unemployment is both systemic and discriminatory. The spread is especially noticeable in Saskatchewan, where non-Aboriginal youth have a lower unemployment rate than Aboriginal people over age twenty-five.

On the plus side, education has been seen by many of our people as key to their future well-being. In the urban areas studied, about one-half to two-thirds of Aboriginal youth between fifteen and twenty-four were attending school in 2001 compared to one-third to one-half in 1981.

The statistical information tells part of the story, but life in the cities for Aboriginal families creates its own problems. Families are often separated from the elders on the reserve. Twice as many Aboriginal children live in single-parent households compared to non-Aboriginal children.

Housing is crowded and substandard, and families are forced into crowded neighbourhoods and apartment buildings, a far cry from the rural lifestyle back on the reserve. Reserve life has its problems, but the cities tend to bring on a poverty of culture and spirit that is harder to combat than material poverty.

Saskatchewan residents now have to realize that all their futures are closely tied together. Aboriginal people are an integral part of this province's economy and politics. Both federal and provincial politicians now agree that Aboriginal issues must be part of their policy platforms and strategies. It was no fluke that Saskatchewan Party leader Brad Wall spent a full day at the last chiefs' legislative assembly in North Battleford.

The rapidly growing urban Aboriginal population will provide Saskatchewan residents with a new workforce. Training and employment are the key to Saskatchewan's next century. The other option is to do nothing and continue to see a portion of the population languish in poverty. With the rapidly increasing Aboriginal population, it is less of an option than ever.

What a Change a Century Makes

On September 4, 1905, Saskatchewan went from being a part of the North-West Territories to having the status of a province. In 1905 Saskatchewan was filled with promise, and the land rush would soon be on as the "empty" land filled with settlers.

What was life like for the First Nations and Métis people in 1905? We were the original inhabitants, but to look at the historical record, we were not considered a serious part of the new province.

In 1905 there were about 12,000 treaty Indians in Saskatchewan; this number dropped to around 9,000 after the influenza epidemic of 1918. It seemed clear to those in government that we were a vanishing race and would not be around in another hundred years.

Back in 1905, things were much different for Aboriginal people. It was twenty years after the resistance of 1885, and many reserves and Métis settlements still felt the repression. Many of the First Nations that participated in the North-West Rebellion were considered "rebel" bands and not allowed to elect chiefs and headmen until well into the 1930s. Of course, unrecognized leadership emerged, and our people continued to practise an internalized form of First Nations and Métis government.

In 1905, life in Indian Country was the best of times and the worst of times, to quote Charles Dickens. Our people were poor and colonized, but they were also hard-working and industrious.

The Indian Act was very strict and clear that Indian culture would not be tolerated. Gatherings were outlawed, and people needed passes to leave the reserve and permission from the Indian agent to sell farm produce. Traditional religious practices were also outlawed. But as is often the case, repression creates stealth, and the traditional Indian religion and culture continued. After Indian agents pulled down the community lodge, people sang and danced in their homes. People left the reserve at will, and there were not enough police to chase them all down. Every so often I hear someone complain that Indians don't respect the law. Is it any wonder? It's part of our history to ignore or break the law.

At this time, our people worked off the reserve and played an important part in the settling of the West. Settlers were arriving in droves and most were hopeless tenderfoots. These were immigrants from Europe or the United States; many had never farmed before, and they needed help. Aboriginal people broke and sold horses to the settlers. They also sold fish, game, and farm produce, fence posts and logs. They worked clearing land and later they worked on threshing crews. Métis teamsters hauled freight across the prairie to the new towns that were springing up.

Because some of the settlers were such hopeless greenhorns, they often lost livestock, and our people were hired to hunt down stray horses and cattle, returning them to the rightful owner. Chickens and pigs also went missing, but they were never returned. Instead, they made some family a welcome feast. Many settlers survived the first hard years largely because of help from First Nations and Métis people.

However, Indians were not seen as a part of the new Saskatchewan. We were seen instead as domestics and farm hands. The residential schools that were built in the 1920s trained our people to cook, herd cattle, and plant gardens. No academic or entrepreneurial skills were seen or expected, in spite of the fact that we had always used our wits to survive.

What a change a century makes. Today any right-thinking individual will see that the First Nations and Métis people are an integral part of the new Saskatchewan. Today, combined, we are almost 20 percent of the population. The vanishing Indian is now a serious threat, or a godsend depending on your point of view.

I suggest we pick things up where we were a century ago when Indian people were partners and helped in the economy and development of the province. It's never too late.

Aboriginal Youth Face Endless "Opportunities"

Young Aboriginal people in Saskatchewan face a very complex and uncertain future. The opportunities are endless. They can join a gang, become addicted, and spend years in jail, or go to university, pursue a career, develop a prosperous business, and marry and create a happy family.

The leap from childhood to adulthood is very difficult for any individual regardless of his or her background, but for Aboriginal youth it is an even more difficult time. As a people, we are going through a period of rapid social and political change. We are far more mobile than in the past, and today half our people live in urban areas. The experiences of today's youth are not the same as their parents'. The growth in gang activity and the abundance of street drugs such as crystal meth have made growing up a dangerous time of life.

Communications and improved transportation have brought urban problems back to the reserve, and drugs and gang activity move back and forth with ease.

Today, our First Nations population is approaching 120,000 in Saskatchewan. Half of the First Nations population is under twenty, and this is placing enormous pressure on leaders and politicians in all governments.

What are priorities for today's youth? It's no secret that a good education is the key to future success. Statistics have shown that Aboriginal people with an education blossom and grow, and the Aboriginal business sector is the fastest-growing sector of the province's economy.

What are the biggest pitfalls for today's youth? Drug addiction and gang violence are the major problems. Gang activity is on the increase, and young people are being pulled into a dead-end world of violence and drugs. While gang members are a small minority in Indian Country, they form a deadly force that alienates young people and limits freedom of choice. Kids in gangs don't go on to university or take a trade. They don't get the good jobs. Theirs is a short, painful career in crime followed by a stretch behind bars or a lifetime of addiction or both.

Gangs are a symptom of our times and socio-economic status. Gang activity is common among dispossessed and alienated groups. It's no wonder that gang activity is also prevalent within Black and Hispanic groups as well. Gangs provide their members with a source of income, protection, and a surrogate family. They fill a need that some young people use to survive.

Gangs and drugs may be a spectacular in-your-face issue that preoccupies the public, but today's youth face another serious problem. It may appear more benign, but it affects more people and is a potential time bomb. It is obesity. Today's young people are too fat. A sedentary lifestyle built around the television and video games combined with a diet of junk food is taking a toll on our kids.

Kids in the city have easy access to the corner store, and stores on reserve are well stocked with junk food. Parents want their children to have a better life than they had, and easy access to cheap food at first appears to be a treat, but in the long run it's a serious threat.

Obesity leads to heart disease and diabetes, which in turn leads to a whole variety of ailments: kidney disease, stroke, loss of limbs, loss of eyesight, and the deterioration of the body. The incidence of diabetes is growing at an alarming rate in Indian Country, and the future for many of today's youth may be one where they are sick, on dialysis, blind, or confined to a wheelchair.

This also does not bode well for the health system. Diabetes is an expensive disease to treat if complications arise. In the future, First Nations health care costs will skyrocket if the incidence of diabetes continues to rise.

On the other hand, diabetes is preventable through exercise and proper diet. It may not appear to have the urgency of some of the other social problems, but in the long run the future health of our people is on the line.

Mark Twain wrote that youth was wasted on the young, and in a way he was right. Growing up for Aboriginal people is a difficult time. It's when you realize the reality of reduced opportunities and diminished expectations. It's a time of endless opportunities, most of them bad.

Making Change Meaningful for Youth

They say meaningful change comes from the community level and from experience and knowledge of the problems and the people. We have had no shortage of well-meaning groups who meddle in our affairs and tell us what is best for us. One of the symptoms of colonialism is the lack of control the colonized experience due to outside forces.

One positive example of meaningful change coming from within is occurring on the Montreal Lake First Nation. The First Nation is undertaking a bold experiment to help youth who are classified as "at risk." The project is designed to help young people learn a useful trade, become self-sufficient, and learn more about their culture and community.

Over the decades, our youth were the collateral damage of colonization. Today, young people, with no direction, low self-esteem, and a lack of useful skills are gravitating toward gangs, addictions, and criminal activity. This is having a serious effect on our communities, our families, and individuals. Each decade has seen an increasing number of alienated people living wasted and unfulfilled lives.

Twelve youth have begun the construction of a log home in the community. When they complete it, they will move in. They have been trained to fell trees and hand scribe each log to fit into the structure.

Years ago, all the people in the community lived in log homes, but over the years "stick houses" replaced the log ones, and log home construction was in danger of becoming a lost art.

For the young people, working in the forest is good for both the body and the soul. Along with the obvious positive effects of exercise and clean air, the work connects them to their culture as Woodland Cree. This is where their people came from, and there is a strong need to reconnect with their roots.

In addition to working with their hands, the youth spend two hours each day in classroom instruction, which includes learning about culture, language, history of their reserve, the colonization process, and genealogy. Our old people say you can't tell where you are going unless you know where you came from.

Genealogy may seem like an odd class for young people, but in a reserve setting it is very important. First Nations have traditionally been groupings of families, and in the past, people would change allegiances and move in with another band if they had a falling out with a local chief or wanted to strengthen family ties through marriage. After the treaties were signed and the reserve system was implemented, band lists became static and families were rarely allowed to move to other reserves. This created a situation where families had to be very careful about intermarriage. Traditionally, the women maintain the family trees and are able to tell a young couple if they are too closely related to be married. By teaching the young people genealogy, they learn where all the families in the community came from and how they are related.

The program is designed to increase the self-esteem of the youth and give them a sense of place and cultural significance. Part of the problem that young people face is a lack of knowledge of their own culture and connection with the land that has sustained their people for generations. Many of today's Aboriginal youth find themselves in a cultural void somewhere between their own community and the modern world.

The students are now hard at work constructing the first log home. When it is completed, it will be theirs. In January, they will build a second home on Little Red River reserve which is shared between Montreal Lake and the Lac La Ronge First Nation.

The next step is where the self-sufficiency comes in. The youth will select a chief and council who will become the managers of a log home construction business. They will be mentored by the Montreal Lake chief and council and develop a business plan. The First Nation plans to contract the construction of a number of log homes from the youth. As well, the Montreal Lake First Nation is located in cottage country, and they are looking at the market outside the reserve.

Saskatchewan First Nations have a median age of twenty years. This means that half of the population of 120,000 is less than twenty years of age. This holds the potential of a significant workforce for Saskatchewan or increasing social problems that will have an impact on the whole province. Now is the time for creative and innovative solutions that can break this cycle and produce self-sufficiency for coming generations.

Residential Schools Haunt Us Still

In Canada, issues aren't solved or addressed right away, they are institutionalized. The Gomery inquiry's tedious plodding resulted in more being spent on the inquiry into the government sponsorship scandal than the amount that was allegedly misspent by the Liberal Party. Meanwhile, Indian Residential School Resolution Canada, a government agency, continues to deny and defer claims from former students who were abused in the residential school system.

The residential school issue has turned from a simple case of providing adequate compensation to students who suffered abuse to an institution that is creating careers for civil servants instead of addressing the real issue.

Residential schools were a black mark against Canada and the nation's Indian policy for almost a century. On one hand, there are individual tales of physical and sexual abuse that must be addressed. But on the other hand, the whole system was so flawed that abuse was an inevitable by-product.

Young children were torn away from their families and sent to institutions far from their homes. The purpose was to remove the children from their pagan parents and teach them to be good Christians and future Canadians. The stories of loneliness and despair are the stuff of legends for First Nations people. These institutions were not like Harrow, Eton, or Upper Canada College. They were not designed to support or preserve a way of life, they were designed to destroy one. The very roots of the residential school concept were wrong, and in the end they were a national disgrace.

Residential school survivors have a legitimate claim for compensation collectively and on an individual basis.

First, the system was fundamentally wrong. It was Canada's worst example of white supremacy. The government and churches believed that they were superior in every way and could quite rightfully take a generation of children away from their homes and raise them in their own image.

Second, the government gave the churches a free hand to run things however they chose. The result was horrible examples of sexual and physical abuse. Residential school staff treated the children as they saw fit without ever having to answer to the parents.

The schools were a magnet for pedophiles, sociopaths, and authoritarian creeps and losers. People who couldn't make it in the outside world gravitated to the comfort of the institutions. Young children far from home with no advocate were vulnerable and easy prey for sexual perverts.

One story my friends have told me was the amount of physical abuse that was routinely administered on the students.

Traditionally, our people, particularly the males, would laugh when they were hurt. It was our way of dealing with pain. Even today, Indians laugh at adversity and thus frustrate cops, jail guards and judges. Our philosophy is that you never let them know you are hurting.

Boys who were punished would take it lightly and not cry out. In order to break an Indian boy, those in charge had to deliver a severe punishment. This was one of the reasons why there was so much physical abuse required to break our people down.

And make no mistake, the philosophy was that Indians had to be broken down so they could be rebuilt as responsible, civilized brown white people. This was beyond simple racism. It was white supremacy, pure and simple. White people tried to break Indians the same way they broke horses, with violence and intimidation.

In many cases our people were broken down and never rebuilt. They had to build themselves up again on their own by going back to their roots. Others spent a lifetime in pain, never achieving their potential and fighting demons of drug and alcohol addiction. It seems that the more intelligent and creative a person was, the more they suffered. I can't help but wonder how much natural talent these institutions destroyed.

Today, Canada is reaping what it sowed, but true to the Canadian bureaucratic tradition the solution has been slow and riddled with complexity.

Saskatchewan had eleven residential schools. Only a small minority of reserves were able to convince the government to build day schools. Some of the old residential schools like File Hills, La Ronge, and Delmas burned down or were closed in the 1940s, but others like Prince Albert, Beauval, Lebret, and Duck Lake remained in service up to the 1980s. The last residential schools were run by local tribal councils, but by then both the concept and the buildings were obsolete.

The government was quick to destroy the old schools, and today only the Prince Albert and Muskowekwan student residences are standing. The Muskowekwan student residence is the last of the old classic brick structures, and it should be preserved as our equivalent to a holocaust museum.

It is estimated that there are 85,000 living residential school survivors, but only 6,500 have sued Canada. The remainder have no interest or are waiting to see the outcome. The court process is expensive and time-consuming. I suspect most are waiting to see what the outcome will be.

The Canadian government has issued a statement of reconciliation that acknowledges the role it played in the residential school fiasco. It is "deeply sorry," and "we need to work together in a healing way." Meanwhile, people wanting compensation or an apology must fill out complex forms. The government has spent $250 million with less than 25 percent going to the victims. The alternative dispute resolution (ADR) approach was supposed to be easier on the victims and less confrontational. So far they have spent $100 million on administrative costs, with $1 million paid in compensation.

The government tried to fossilize the process in the hope that there would be so many roadblocks that residential school survivors would give up in frustration. The government strategy here is not justice but justice delayed and hence justice denied.

The Harper government finally agreed to recognize the compensation formula that had been worked out by the previous government. The compensation formula had received all-party support previously so it would have been very difficult to go back on a prior agreement.

Compensation is only a part of the healing equation. The federal Aboriginal Healing Foundation must be renewed and counselling and other assistance made available to residential school survivors. Monetary compensation may satisfy the government lawyers, but we still need a long period of healing and reconciliation.

Profile – Tom Cogwagee Longboat

The name Tom Longboat draws immediate respect in Indian Country. The top Aboriginal amateur athlete each year receives the Tom Longboat Award in recognition of his or her drive and success. The legacy of this famous runner lives on as it should.

Longboat was born in 1887 on the Six Nations reserve near Brantford, Ontario. He was a member of the Onondaga nation, and his Indian name was Cogwagee. Throughout his life he would use his Indian name, and he never turned his back on his people or his heritage.

His father died when he was young, and his mother was left to raise four children by herself. Tom was often seen running on the reserve. He loved to run long distances, and when he was nineteen he entered the Hamilton Bay race. He was an unknown and the odds on him were sixty to one.

Throughout his life he had to deal with the rampant racism of the time. If he didn't win he was a "lazy Indian." If he won he was the "speedy son of the forest." The newspapers called him "Injun" or "Heap Big Chief." It was no surprise that when he competed in his first race the local reporter described him as "a pathetic figure in a pair of bathing trunks with cheap sneakers on his feet, and hair that looked as if it had been hacked off with a tomahawk." Tom went on to win the race and came within a shadow of the course record.

A few days later he won the twenty-four kilometre Ward Marathon in Toronto and several months later won the Boston Marathon with a time of

2:24:20 4/5. This record would stand until the course was changed and made easier.

Longboat had an enormous reserve of strength. During the last mile of the marathon, he would gain speed and sprint to the finish. This would leave his competition in the dust and demoralized.

He became a hero in Canada. He was now a hot property and was under contract to Tom Flanagan, the owner of the Irish Canadian Athletic Club. For a while, Longboat's career continued to flourish, but the strain began to show. Flanagan was domineering and manipulative.

In 1907, the New England Amateur Athletic Union stripped Longboat of his amateur status. He was banned from returning to Boston to defend his title. However, he was able to be a part of the Canadian Olympic team and participate in the 1908 Olympics in London, England. Unfortunately, he collapsed at the nineteen-mile mark and was in second place. The speculation turned to drugs; even the manager of the Canadian Olympic team mused that it must have been a drug overdose. Others speculated that he was drugged so the bookies could rake in a huge windfall. Others pointed to the exceptional heat on the day of the race as being the main factor.

In the end, Longboat left Flanagan, his condescending manager, and did quite well on his own in spite of Flanagan's dark threats that he would squander his winnings and end up in the gutter. After all, he was only an Indian.

Longboat went on to win the most famous race of his career in 1908 at Madison Square Garden. It was a two-man race against Dorando Pietri, the great Italian runner. They raced on a circular track for the full distance of the marathon. The two ran beside each other for the first forty kilometres, with Pietri taking the lead. However, in the last mile Longboat surged ahead in his trademark style. Pietri couldn't keep up, and he collapsed on the track.

For their trouble they were each guaranteed a quarter of the gate, which amounted to $3,750 apiece.

In 1916, at the age of twenty-nine, he joined the army and went to Europe. He was a member of the 107th Pioneer Battalion in France, and he had the dangerous assignment of running messages and orders between units. During this time, he also raced in inter-battalion sports contests. He was wounded twice, and once he was declared dead. He survived the war and returned to Canada in 1919.

He returned to the reserve and married a woman there. For the last twenty years of his life, he worked as a garbage collector in Toronto. The Canadian public largely forgot him, but his fame lived on with his own people.

He died in 1947 of pneumonia brought on by diabetes. He was buried on Six Nations. The funeral service was conducted in the Native spiritual tradition, a tradition he held to throughout his life.

Today he remains a special hero to Indians on both sides of the border. People mention his name with respect and take pride in his legacy.

Profile – Harry Cook

In March 2005, Harry Cook left his position as chief of the Lac La Ronge band after twenty-one years of service to the band, three as a band councillor and eighteen as the chief.

The Lac La Ronge Indian Band is the largest First Nation in the province, consisting of 7,700 members spread over six northern communities. The past several decades have seen enormous changes in Northern Saskatchewan, and the Lac La Ronge band has been at the forefront of those changes.

For example, today 60 percent of the band's population is under the age of twenty-five. This has forced the band government to place an emphasis on education and employment. One of Chief Cook's priorities was to build schools for all the communities. Today, all of the six communities have good-quality schools.

I asked Chief Cook what he saw as one of the biggest accomplishments of his term in office. He said that before he went into politics he was the band's housing coordinator. At that time only community buildings like schools and the band office had water and sewer. Over his term as chief, he would see that all six communities received the proper infrastructure, including water and sewer services provided by the band.

But throughout the province, economic development was Chief Cook's biggest legacy. The Kitsaki Development Corporation is one of the largest Aboriginal companies in Canada. Together with various joint venture partners they have ownership in the following companies:

- Northern Resource Trucking, which serves the northern mines as well as bulk fuel and logging subsidiary companies
- Athabasca Catering also serves the northern mines, providing food services
- Wapawekka Lumber, a sawmill operation that is surviving in spite of the high tariffs on softwood lumber in the American market
- First Nations Insurance Services provides pensions and benefits for Saskatchewan First Nations, and six of the seven-person staff are First Nations
- Northern Lights Foods, consisting of a meat processing plant as well as marketing for wild rice and native mushrooms, provides part-time work to around one thousand people in seasonal jobs of wild rice and mushroom picking.
- Canada North Environmental Services provides environmental monitoring and consulting services to the mining and construction sector
- A one-sixth share of the Dakota Dunes Golf Course on the Whitecap First Nation

Other economic ventures by the band include the La Ronge Motor Inn, the band's gas bar, grocery store, and lumberyard, and Keethanow Bingo North. The bingo provides money for band projects including sports and recreation and the band "emergency fund" that provides money for hospital visits for remote band members and other emergencies.

In total, Kitsaki employs about five hundred people. One-third are band members, one-third are from other First Nations, and the remaining third are from the general population.

But in spite of all the band's success, Harry Cook remains a humble man. He told me that it takes strong families to build a community and that is what he stresses to each band member.

Chief Cook is only sixty-one, so his retirement will be from politics only. He plans to maintain his seat on the Cameco board of directors and his position on an advisory committee for the minister of International Trade and Commerce. "It's important that we work within the bigger society," he told me. In addition, he plans to do economic and political consulting and other work which may come up.

One of the other reasons for his retirement from politics was to spend more time with his wife and family and in his words, "take care of myself." About ten years ago he was diagnosed with diabetes, and the tough life of politics with all the travel and meetings took its toll. The morning I spoke to him, he was about to jump on his snow machine and travel forty-eight kilometres to visit a friend on his trapline. "I couldn't do this before," he told me.

ACKNOWLEDGEMENTS

I would like to thank my dad, Dr. Stan Cuthand. Dad was a professor of Native Studies, and taught at the University of Manitoba and the First Nations University of Canada. Throughout his life he was active in First Nations politics and frequently translated at political gatherings. But he was first and foremost a minister in the Anglican Church and over the years he helped many people at a time before the political organizations and social programs even existed.

I would also like to thank the Saskatoon *StarPhoenix* and the Regina *Leader-Post,* who have published my columns for the past 15 years. (My column total is about 750, saved on four computers.)

I would also like to thank the Canada Council for its financial assistance during the creation of the *Askiwina* manuscript.

But most of all I would like to thank my wife and family, who have always been there for me, especially during the dark days of the past year. In June, 2006, we lost our beloved son Christopher, and it is to his memory that I dedicate this book.

ABOUT THE AUTHOR

Doug Cuthand is an independent film producer, director, writer and journalist whose career has spanned over 20 years. His work has been recognized and honoured by the media industry.

Weekly columns in the Saskatoon *StarPhoenix* and Regina *Leader-Post,* as well as features in the *Winnipeg Free Press* and other print media, have made Mr. Cuthand a respected voice for the aboriginal community. A collection of his newspaper writings was published in 2005 as *Tapwe.*

Doug Cuthand lives with his family in Saskatoon.

ABOUT THE ARTIST

Jerry Whitehead is a Cree native from the James Smith Band, Saskatchewan. Jerry obtained his formal art training in Saskatchewan and Nova Scotia. He has been involved in various activities as an exhibition coordinator, workshop leader, illustrator, and teaching assistant.

Throughout Jerry's career, his artwork has gone through a number of stages. However, the one thing that has remained constant throughout this progression is his focus on powwows and powwow dancers. Today, Jerry produces abstract paintings of vivid color, incorporating family themes and words in his pieces.

Jerry's works have been exhibited throughout Canada and hang in various countries. He currently resides in Vancouver, British Columbia with his family.

MEMBER OF SCABRINI GROUP

Québec, Canada
2007